DEBRA MURRAY'S BEST
Pressure Cooker
Book Ever

ACKNOWLEDGMENTS

I AM SO BLESSED TO BE ABLE TO HAVE THE JOB OF MY DREAMS PLAYING WITH COOKING PRODUCTS. My most beloved cooking product being an electric pressure cooker. I hope this book inspires you to pressure cook!

I would like to thank my village of angels who encourage and inspire me every day!

Thank you Mark Linduski for hiring me, and finding me wonderful products to demonstrate. I truly appreciate all your love and support. I will never be able to repay your kindness.

I must thank my beautiful daughter Nevar; you are not only beautiful, but smart and fun! You are my best friend! Thanks for always encouraging me! I am so blessed to have the best mom, dad, sister, and bonus mom, Myrna. Thanks for all your love and support!

I want to thank Bob McGeeney for the brilliant products he designs for me. I adore your passion and enthusiasm. Keep up the great designs!

I want to thank Chris Davis my brilliant and ever-so-talented photographer (inset). This is the 10th book Chris and I have done together. He is not only super talented as an artist, but one of the best people I have ever known! Diane Linder for editing this book, goodness knows I so need you! Thank you to Josephine Cook for promoting all my shows and being such a dear friend! Thanks to my brilliant assistant Shannon Kelly, and my pressure cooker food stylist and friend Pati Lippka thanks for sharing my passion and your gorgeous food! Thank you to Michele Trombley my book designer, your work and patience are commendable!

But most of all I would like to thank my best friend, Laurie Bain (inset). I could not have done it without you my friend! She typed, tested, food-styled, and just has been there for me like no one else…love you buddy!

Chris and Laurie Bain at work.

3

TABLE OF CONTENTS

INTRODUCTION

I Debra Murray have a passion for pressure cooking! I feel it is my reason for being alive.

I have been madly in love with pressure cooking since my first hands-on experience with one almost 20 years ago. One bite of pot roast, and I became a loyal fan.

The reason I am so crazy for pressure cooking has nothing to do with the ease or speed of cooking (both of which are substantial). I love the flavor and textures.

What happens in a pressure cooker is when the cooking liquid comes to a boil, the water temperature is 212 degrees. At that point, water is converted to a vapor (or steam). When the steam is prevented from escaping, it raises the temperature of the cooking liquid by 40 degrees. That in itself would help to cut back on the cooking time. But the steam molecules also help to break down the surface tension of whatever you are cooking and infuses the food with the flavors of the cooking liquid. So the flavors are more intense. For instance, roasting a piece of beef or cooking it in a slow cooker will taste much different than that of a beef cooked in the pressure cooker. If you use wine, the meat will boost that attribute; or if using stock and herbs, you will clearly taste them throughout.

I did a cooking class at my church once, and I merely made sliced carrots in the pressure cooker using a little chicken stock for the steam. The look on the face of every person that tasted them was amazement. I did a butternut squash half as well with a touch of rosemary; again the shock on all the tasters' faces was amazing.

I make everything quick and easy; from one pot pasta using dry noodles and frozen protein, to rice and beans and meats. But my favorite still is the stocks and soups.

I have over 100 recipes here for you to start on the road to pressure cooking, because if you don't love pressure cooking, you obviously have never tried it.

I have included a tips section, a cooking chart, and a great pantry list.

I have written this book for my beloved Cook's Companion Ceramic Pressure Cooker and Yogurt maker; however, most electric pressure cookers maintain the same temperature inside. You will just need to make sure you set yours for the correct amount of time to be under pressure.

Thanks in advance for your purchase! If you have questions you can always leave me a message on my web page, www.debramurraycooking.com.

TIPS

IF YOU HAVE NEVER EXPERIENCED FOOD MADE IN A PRESSURE COOKER, YOU ARE ABOUT TO BE AMAZED. As a young girl my grandmother had all kinds of pressure cookers. We had an enormous garden where we gathered and canned fruits and vegetables all summer so that we could enjoy them all winter. My grandmother always cooked the vegetables in the pressure cooker. Beets, tomatoes, green beans — they were always so delicious.

I had not thought of pressure cooking when I started a family of my own. When a friend gave me a stove top pressure cooker some 20 years ago, it started a real love story.

I have found that braised meats like pot roasts or briskets not only cook in less than half the time, but I also like the flavor better. The steam tenderizes the meat without the need of fat and locks in the vitamins, nutrients and colors. The pressure cooker infuses the flavors and produces even more flavorful meats than roasting. Vegetables are cooked to perfection in minutes.

Other advantages of the pressure cooking are less electricity, not heating up the house or filling the home with cooking smells.

The programmable pressure cooker is by far the best for safety, ease of use and design. It lets me cook an even larger variety of foods than I would be able to with a stove top pressure cooker. Most stove top pressure cookers discourage cooking pasta or apple sauce, but with the electric ones you can cook anything.

Here is a list of tips to help you get the most from your pressure cooker.

* It is very important to have a liquid such as water, stock, juice, or wine in the pressure cooker in order to create steam. Thicker sauces such as barbecue or tomato sauce will not create steam. At least ¼ – ½ cup are necessary to create adequate steam.

* Each function has its own specific temperature and pressure. A suggested function may not be exactly the foods you are cooking, and may seem odd to you, but I chose it because it achieved the best results.

* When cooking a rice, bean or pasta dish, do not fill the pressure cooker more than halfway. When cooking soup or stocks, do not exceed the ⅔ mark.

* You should carefully wash the lid and remove the regulator for cleaning. The valves and regulator need to be cleaned for the pressure cooker to operate properly.

* I do not recommend using the quick release method for letting the pressure out unless the recipe calls for adding additional ingredients. Some recipes, like rice for instance, need the extra time from letting it slowly release on its own to absorb and finish the cooking process. Also, remember to never attempt to open the lid while pressure cooker is in progress. Wait until the pressure is fully vented before opening lid.

* If you live in higher altitudes, you may increase the cooking times slightly. I suggest adding 5% cooking time for every 1000 feet above sea level.

* All the recipes were tested by weight so if you wish to cook a larger piece of meat, you will need to increase the cooking time. Add 10 minutes to the suggested cooking time for every additional pound of meat.

* If your meat is not as tender as you would like it, simply add ½ cup of liquid and increase the cook time by 10 minutes. Meat is not graded or marbled with the same amount of fat, so there may be some fluctuation in cooking times.

CHART

IF YOU EVER COMPLETE A RECIPE AND THE COOKING LIQUID IS THINNER THAN YOU DESIRE, simply press the brown/saute function and let the liquid reduce with the lid off until the desired consistency is achieved.

Please use the chart below for your reference:

INGREDIENT	AMOUNT	FUNCTION	TIME SUGGESTED (Minutes)	LIQUID (Cups)
VEGETABLES				
Artichokes, trimmed	3 med	Fish/Vegetables	14	2
Beans, Black	1 cup	Fish/Vegetables	12	2
Beans, Navy	1 cup	Fish/Vegetables	8	2 – 2 ½
Beans, Pinto	1 cup	Rice	15	3
Beans, Red Kidney	1 cup	Rice	20	3 ½
Beans, String	1 lb	Fish/Vegetables	3	1
Beets	6 med	Fish/Vegetables	15	2
Cabbage Head, quartered	1 med	Fish/Vegetables	10	2
Carrots, 2" pieces	2 cups	Fish/Vegetables	5	1
Corn on the Cob	6 ears	Fish/Vegetables	4	1 ½
Parsnips, cubed	2 cups	Fish/Vegetables	4	1 ½
Squash, Acorn, halved	4 halves	Fish/Vegetables	13	2
Squash, Butternut ½" slices	8 slices	Fish/Vegetables	4	1 ½
MEATS, POULTRY, SEAFOOD				
Beef Brisket	3 lbs	Meat/Poultry	90	2 – 3
Beef Ribs	6 whole	Meat/Poultry	30	2
Chicken, boneless, skinless pieces, frozen	4 lbs	Meat/Poultry	5	2

Continued on page 10

Chicken, legs	4 whole	Meat/Poultry	20	2
Chicken, quartered	1 whole	Meat/Poultry	20	2
Chicken, whole	3 lbs	Meat/Poultry	20	3
Chuck Roast	3 lbs	Meat/Poultry	75	2 – 3
Corned Beef	3 lbs	Meat/Poultry	90	3
Baby Back Ribs	2 slabs	Meat/Poultry	20	2
Lamb Shanks	2 – 3 lbs	Meat/Poultry	30	2
Pork Chops (8-10 oz each)	3 – 4	Meat/Poultry	12	2
Pork Loin	2 lbs	Meat/Poultry	22	3
Short Ribs	3 lbs	Meat/Poultry	35	2
Spare Ribs	1 slab	Meat/Poultry	30	2
Stew Meat 1" pieces	3 lbs	Meat/Poultry	18	4
Turkey Breast	5 lbs	Meat/Poultry	45	3
Veal Shanks (8 oz each)	3	Meat/Poultry	30	2
POTATOES				
Potato, Baking	4 large	Fish/Vegetables	15	2
Potatoes, Red Bliss	up to 20	Fish/Vegetables	7	2
Potatoes, White, cubed	3 cups	Fish/Vegetables	5	½

SAVORY SOUPS AND STEWS
TO WARM THE SOUL

Beef Bourguignon Stew

Servings: 6

INGREDIENTS

2 tablespoons extra-virgin olive oil

2 pound chuck roast, cut into ½-inch pieces

1 teaspoon sea salt

½ teaspoon freshly ground pepper

8 ounces baby Portobello mushrooms, sliced

1 cup beef stock

1 cup pearl onions

4 garlic cloves

3 sprigs fresh thyme

2 tablespoons black currant jelly

¼ cup crushed tomatoes

2 carrots, peeled and sliced into 2-inch pieces

DIRECTIONS

1. Press brown/sauté function; add oil and preheat.
2. Season meat with salt and pepper.
3. Add the meat to the pressure cooker and sear for 2 minutes on each side.
4. Remove meat to a platter and cover.
5. Add mushrooms to the pressure cooker and cook for 3 minutes; stir occasionally.
6. Add the stock to de-glaze the pressure cooker; scrape up all the little bits from the bottom.
7. Add remaining ingredients to the pressure cooker; secure lid.
8. Press soup function, add 5 minutes; press start.
9. When cook time is complete, and pressure is fully vented, open lid.
10. Remove and discard the thyme sprigs and serve.

NUTRITION FACTS

Serving Size:
1/6 of a recipe.

Amount Per Serving	% Daily Value
Calories: 99	5%
Calories from Fat: 51	8%
Total Fat: 6g	9%
Saturated Fat: 1g	5%
Cholesterol: 12mg	4%
Sodium: 488mg	20%
Total Carbohydrates: 6g	2%
Fiber: 0g	0%
Sugars: 4g	
Protein: 6g	11%
Vitamin A:	0%
Vitamin C:	1%
Calcium:	0%
Iron:	2%

Pork & Apple Stew

Servings: 6

INGREDIENTS

2 tablespoons extra-virgin olive oil

1 pork loin roast (1 ½ pounds) cut into 2-inch chunks

1 teaspoon salt

1 teaspoon freshly ground pepper

½ teaspoon fennel seeds

1 teaspoon rosemary leaves

1 cup chicken stock

2 Granny Smith apples, peeled, cored, sliced and divided

1 cup purple cabbage, shredded

6 red bliss potatoes, washed and halved

DIRECTIONS

1. Press brown/sauté function, add oil and preheat.
2. Season pork with salt, pepper, fennel, and rosemary.
3. Add the pork to the pressure cooker and sear for 2 minutes on each side.
4. Transfer pork to a platter and cover.
5. Add chicken stock to deglaze the pressure cooker; scrape up all the little bits from the bottom.
6. Add pork and half the apples to the pressure cooker; secure lid.
7. Press bake function; press start.
8. When cook time is complete, and pressure is fully vented, open lid.
9. Add the cabbage, potatoes, and remaining apples to the pressure cooker; secure lid.
10. Press fish function; press start.
11. When cook time is complete, and pressure is fully vented, open lid.
12. Serve immediately.

TIP

Serve with a touch of cider vinegar.

NUTRITION FACTS

Serving Size:
1/6 of a recipe.

Amount Per Serving	% Daily Value
Calories: 582	29%
Calories from Fat: 226	34%
Total Fat: 26g	40%
Saturated Fat: 10g	50%
Cholesterol: 210mg	70%
Sodium: 810mg	33%
Total Carbohydrates: 0g	0%
Fiber: 0g	0%
Sugars: 0g	
Protein: 90g	164%
Vitamin A:	0%
Vitamin C:	0%
Calcium:	0%
Iron:	9%

Creamy Chicken & Dumpling Soup

Servings: 6

INGREDIENTS

4 boneless skinless chicken breasts

2 tablespoons extra-virgin olive oil

½ teaspoon kosher salt

½ teaspoon salt

¼ teaspoon freshly ground pepper

1 teaspoon poultry seasoning

½ cup white wine

5 cups of chicken stock

2 celery stalks, cut into 1-inch pieces

2 carrots, peeled and cut into 1-inch slices

1 leek (white part only) thinly sliced

2 garlic cloves

1 sprig fresh thyme

1 ¼ cups unbleached all-purpose flour

2 teaspoons baking powder

1 large egg, beaten

1 tablespoon butter, melted

½ cup Half & Half

¼ teaspoon dried sage

1 teaspoon dried parsley

DIRECTIONS

1. Cut chicken into 1-inch pieces and pat dry using paper towels.
2. Press brown/ sauté function; add oil and preheat.
3. Place chicken into pressure cooker.
4. Season the chicken with kosher salt, pepper, and poultry seasoning; brown the chicken on each side.
5. Remove chicken to a platter and cover.
6. Add wine to de-glaze the pressure cooker; scrape up all the little bits from the bottom.
7. Add remaining soup ingredients to the pressure cooker; secure lid.
8. Press rice function, minus 2 minutes; press start.
9. While soup is cooking, combine flour, baking powder, salt, sage, egg, butter, Half & Half and parsley into a bowl; do not overmix.
10. When cook time is complete, and pressure is fully vented, open lid.
11. Remove and discard the thyme sprig.
12. With the lid off, press brown/ sauté function.
13. When soup simmers, drop small dumplings into the soup using a teaspoon until all the batter has been used.
14. Carefully turn dumplings using a teaspoon, cook through and serve.

NUTRITION FACTS

Serving Size:
1/6 of a recipe.

Amount Per Serving	% Daily Value
Calories: 300	20%
Calories from Fat: 70	11%
Total Fat: 8g	12%
Saturated Fat: 1g	5%
Cholesterol: 29mg	10%
Sodium: 800mg	33%
Total Carbohydrates: 28g	9%
Fiber: 3g	12%
Sugars: 0g	
Protein: 6g	11%
Vitamin A:	2%
Vitamin C:	20%
Calcium:	6%
Iron:	5%

Cajun Bean Soup

Servings: 8

INGREDIENTS

1 pound 15 bean soup mix

1 large onion, diced

1 can (28 ounces) crushed tomatoes

3 stalks of celery, chopped

1 ham hock

1 pound of pork shoulder, diced into 1-inch cubes

2 garlic cloves, minced

1 tablespoon parsley

1 teaspoon rosemary

2 teaspoons salt

1 teaspoon black pepper

¼ teaspoon cayenne pepper

8 cups of chicken stock

1 sprig thyme

DIRECTIONS

1. Place all ingredients into the pressure cooker; secure lid.
2. Press soup function, add 5 minutes; press start.
3. When cook time is complete, and pressure is fully vented, open lid.
4. Remove ham hock and sprig thyme.
5. Serve immediately.

NUTRITION FACTS

Serving Size:
1/8 of a recipe.

Amount Per Serving	% Daily Value
Calories: 240	25%
Calories from Fat: 21	3%
Total Fat: 3g	5%
Saturated Fat: 0g	0%
Cholesterol: 655mg	218%
Sodium: 110mg	4%
Total Carbohydrates: 80g	27%
Fiber: 0g	0%
Sugars: 0g	
Protein: 217g	395%
Vitamin A:	0%
Vitamin C:	5%
Calcium:	19%
Iron:	21%

Chicken Noodle Soup

Servings: 8

INGREDIENTS

1 (5 pound) whole chicken

4 cups water

2 teaspoons sea salt

1 teaspoon turmeric powder

½ teaspoon black pepper

1 sprig fresh thyme

1 leek (white part only) halved

2 garlic cloves

2 celery stalks, cut into 2-inch pieces

2 whole carrots, peeled and cut into 2-inch pieces

½ cup dry egg noodles

1 tablespoon flat leaf parsley, chopped

DIRECTIONS

1. Place all ingredients, except celery, carrots, noodles and parsley, into the pressure cooker; secure lid.
2. Press soup function, add five minutes; press start.
3. When cook time is complete, and pressure is fully vented, open lid.
4. Strain the pressure cooker contents through a sieve into a container.
5. Refrigerate the stock for 30 minutes.
6. Remove the chicken meat from the bones, place the meat back into the pressure cooker and discard the bones.
7. Remove the stock from the refrigerator, remove and discard the hardened fat from the top, then pour it back into the pressure cooker.
8. Add remaining ingredients to the pressure cooker; secure lid.
9. Press fish function; press start.
10. When cook time is complete, and pressure is fully vented, open lid.
11. Serve immediately.

NUTRITION FACTS

Serving Size:
1/8 of a recipe.

Amount Per Serving	% Daily Value
Calories: 128	6%
Calories from Fat: 4	1%
Total Fat: 0g	0%
Saturated Fat: 0g	0%
Cholesterol: 17mg	6%
Sodium: 400mg	22%
Total Carbohydrates: 10g	3%
Fiber: 3g	12%
Sugars: 0g	
Protein: 8g	15%
Vitamin A:	0%
Vitamin C:	20%
Calcium:	5%
Iron:	2%

Lobster Asparagus Soup

Servings: 6

INGREDIENTS

2 cups chicken stock

1 cup white wine

1 lemon, halved

1 leek (white part only) sliced

1 stalk of celery

2 lobster tails, with shells

1 teaspoon lemon pepper seasoning

1 pound fresh asparagus, cut into 1-inch pieces

4 ounces of cream cheese

DIRECTIONS

1. Place all ingredients, except cream cheese, into the pressure cooker; secure lid.
2. Press rice function, minus 2 minutes; press start.
3. When cook time is complete, and pressure is fully vented, open lid.
4. Remove lobster meat from tails and discard shells.
5. Cut lobster meat into ½-inch pieces and place them back into pressure cooker.
6. Add cream cheese to the pressure cooker and stir until dissolved.
7. Serve hot or cold.

NUTRITION FACTS

Serving Size:
1/6 of a recipe.

Amount Per Serving	% Daily Value
Calories: 227	11%
Calories from Fat: 95	14%
Total Fat: 11g	17%
Saturated Fat: 6g	30%
Cholesterol: 33mg	11%
Sodium: 963mg	20%
Total Carbohydrates: 23g	8%
Fiber: 4g	16%
Sugars: 0g	
Protein: 11g	20%
Vitamin A:	17%
Vitamin C:	11%
Calcium:	0%
Iron:	0%

Fish Stock

Servings: 8

INGREDIENTS

2 pounds snapper or grouper fish heads

1 medium onion, quartered

1 celery stalk

1 small carrot

2 sprigs thyme

6 whole peppercorns

½ tablespoon kosher salt

4 cups water

DIRECTIONS

1. Place all ingredients into the pressure cooker; secure lid.
2. Press meat function; press start.
3. When cook time is complete, and pressure is fully vented, open lid.
4. Strain the stock using a colander.
5. Cover and refrigerate.
6. Stock will keep refrigerated for up to 7 days.

NUTRITION FACTS

Serving Size:
1/8 of a recipe.

Amount Per Serving	% Daily Value
Calories: 200	22%
Calories from Fat: 0	0%
Total Fat: 0g	0%
Saturated Fat: 0g	0%
Cholesterol: 0mg	0%
Sodium: 460mg	23%
Total Carbohydrates: 1g	0%
Fiber: 0g	0%
Sugars: 0g	
Protein: 0g	0%
Vitamin A:	0%
Vitamin C:	5%
Calcium:	0%
Iron:	0%

Lentils with Italian Sausage

Servings: 8

INGREDIENTS

1 pound sweet Italian sausage, cut into 1-inch pieces

1 medium onion, diced

2 garlic cloves, sliced

1 large carrot, peeled and thinly sliced

1 celery stalk, thinly sliced

1 cup lentils

2 cups chicken stock

1 can (14.5 ounces) diced tomatoes with garlic and olive oil

1 bay leaf

½ teaspoon crushed red pepper flakes (optional)

DIRECTIONS

1. Place all ingredients into the pressure cooker; secure lid.
2. Press meat function, add 5 minutes; press start.
3. When cook time is complete, and pressure is fully vented, open lid.
4. Remove bay leaf and serve.

NUTRITION FACTS

Serving Size:
1/8 of a recipe.

Amount Per Serving	% Daily Value
Calories: 210	19%
Calories from Fat: 235	35%
Total Fat: 26g	40%
Saturated Fat: 9g	45%
Cholesterol: 65mg	22%
Sodium: 370mg	20%
Total Carbohydrates: 22g	7%
Fiber: 9g	36%
Sugars: 0g	
Protein: 3g	5%
Vitamin A:	0%
Vitamin C:	5%
Calcium:	0%
Iron:	19%

French Onion Soup

Servings: 4

INGREDIENTS

4 large sweet onions, sliced

2 cups beef stock

1 tablespoon balsamic vinegar

¼ cup red wine

2 sprigs thyme

1 bay leaf

½ teaspoon salt

½ teaspoon freshly ground black pepper

8 ounces of Gruyere cheese, sliced

DIRECTIONS

1. Place all ingredients, except cheese, into the pressure cooker; secure lid.

2. Press meat function, add 5 minutes; press start.

3. When cook time is complete, and pressure is fully vented, open lid.

4. Remove thyme and bay leaf.

5. Turn oven on to broil.

6. Ladle soup into oven safe bowls, then top each bowl with 2 slices of cheese.

7. Place bowls under the broiler for 2 minutes or until cheese is melted.

8. Serve immediately.

NUTRITION FACTS

Serving Size:
1/4 of a recipe.

Amount Per Serving	% Daily Value
Calories: 220	20%
Calories from Fat: 33	5%
Total Fat: 4g	6%
Saturated Fat: 1g	5%
Cholesterol: 37mg	12%
Sodium: 475mg	20%
Total Carbohydrates: 1g	0%
Fiber: 0g	0%
Sugars: 1g	
Protein: 13g	24%
Vitamin A:	0%
Vitamin C:	0%
Calcium:	0%
Iron:	8%

Ginger Carrot Soup

Servings: 6

INGREDIENTS

6 large carrots, peeled and chopped

1 medium onion, diced

2 tablespoons fresh ginger, minced

2 cups of chicken stock

½ cup of orange juice

1 teaspoon salt

½ teaspoon freshly ground pepper

DIRECTIONS

1. Place all ingredients into the pressure cooker; secure lid.
2. Press fish function; press start.
3. When cook time is complete, and pressure is fully vented, open lid.
4. Puree soup in a blender and serve.

NUTRITION FACTS

Serving Size:
1/6 of a recipe.

Amount Per Serving	% Daily Value
Calories: 150	15%
Calories from Fat: 5	1%
Total Fat: 1g	2%
Saturated Fat: 0g	0%
Cholesterol: 0mg	0%
Sodium: 215mg	15%
Total Carbohydrates: 6g	2%
Fiber: 0g	0%
Sugars: 4g	
Protein: 3g	5%
Vitamin A:	0%
Vitamin C:	21%
Calcium:	1%
Iron:	0%

Greek Lemon Chicken Soup

Servings: 8

INGREDIENTS

6 cups chicken stock

2 boneless skinless chicken breasts

1 teaspoon freshly ground pepper

1 teaspoon turmeric powder

1 teaspoon salt

1 bay leaf

1 teaspoon lemon zest

1 medium onion, chopped

1 celery stalk, sliced

1 carrot, peeled and sliced

¼ cup quinoa, rinsed

½ cup lemon juice

2 large eggs, beaten

1 egg yolk, beaten

2 tablespoons mint leaves, chopped

DIRECTIONS

1. Place all ingredients except quinoa, lemon juice, eggs, yolk and mint leaves, into the pressure cooker; secure lid.
2. Press meat function, add 5 minutes; press start.
3. When cook time is complete, and pressure is fully vented, open lid.
4. Pour the pressure cooker contents through a strainer, separating the stock from the chicken and vegetables.
5. Pour the stock back into the pressure cooker.
6. Discard all the vegetables and chop the chicken; set aside.
7. Add the quinoa to the pressure cooker.
8. Press brown/sauté function; cook for 5 minutes with lid off.
9. When cooking is complete, combine lemon juice, eggs and yolk in a bowl; whisk well.
10. Ladle ¼ cup of hot stock into the egg mixture; whisk well.
11. Drizzle the egg mixture into the pressure cooker while continuously whisking.
12. Add the chicken and mint to the pressure cooker.
13. Cook for an additional 3 minutes before serving. Serve immediately.

NUTRITION FACTS

Serving Size:
1/8 of a recipe.

Amount Per Serving	% Daily Value
Calories: 129	10%
Calories from Fat: 19	3%
Total Fat: 2g	3%
Saturated Fat: 0g	0%
Cholesterol: 48mg	16%
Sodium: 400mg	15%
Total Carbohydrates: 2g	1%
Fiber: 0g	0%
Sugars: 0g	
Protein: 6g	11%
Vitamin A:	1%
Vitamin C:	3%
Calcium:	0%
Iron:	1%

Hot Sour Noodle Soup with Shrimp

Servings: 8

INGREDIENTS

5 cups chicken stock

4 garlic cloves, sliced

1 tablespoon fresh ginger, grated

1 star anise

3 tablespoons fish sauce

1 tablespoon soy sauce

1 teaspoon brown sugar

1 serrano chili pepper, seeds and membrane removed, thinly sliced

1 lemongrass stalk, halved

1 teaspoon lime zest

1 pound shrimp, peeled and deveined

2 cups bean sprouts

2 green onions, cut into 1-inch pieces

2 tablespoons cilantro leaves, chopped

2 tablespoons fresh mint leaves, chopped

6 ounces rice noodles, cooked

DIRECTIONS

1. Place all ingredients, except rice noodles, into the pressure cooker; secure lid.
2. Press rice function, minus 2 minutes; press start.
3. When cook time is complete, and pressure is fully vented, open lid.
4. Remove lemongrass, then add the rice noodles to pressure cooker; stir.
5. Divide the soup between bowls and serve.

NUTRITION FACTS

Serving Size:
1/8 of a recipe.

Amount Per Serving	% Daily Value
Calories: 140	8%
Calories from Fat: 54	8%
Total Fat: 6g	9%
Saturated Fat: 1g	5%
Cholesterol: 151mg	50%
Sodium: 1000mg	50%
Total Carbohydrates: 41g	14%
Fiber: 0g	0%
Sugars: 5g	
Protein: 23g	42%
Vitamin A:	15%
Vitamin C:	136%
Calcium:	2%
Iron:	23%

Kabocha Squash Soup

Servings: 6

INGREDIENTS

1 (2.5 pound) kabocha squash, peeled, seeded and cut into 2-inch pieces

2 cups chicken stock

1 small onion, chopped

3 garlic cloves, sliced

1 teaspoon salt

1 teaspoon freshly ground pepper

2 tablespoons ginger, sliced

¼ cup orange juice

1 tablespoon brown sugar

DIRECTIONS

1. Place all ingredients except basil, into the pressure cooker; secure lid.
2. Press rice function, minus 2 minutes; press start.
3. When cook time is complete, and pressure is fully vented, open lid.
4. Puree soup using immersion blender until desired consistency and serve.

TIP

Garnish with sour cream and cranberry sauce.

NUTRITION FACTS

Serving Size:
1/6 of a recipe.

Amount Per Serving	% Daily Value
Calories: 288	20%
Calories from Fat: 5	1%
Total Fat: 2g	3%
Saturated Fat: 0g	0%
Cholesterol: 0mg	0%
Sodium: 196mg	5%
Total Carbohydrates: 35g	12%
Fiber: 6g	24%
Sugars: 5g	
Protein: 5g	9%
Vitamin A:	0%
Vitamin C:	13%
Calcium:	1%
Iron:	0%

Pizza Soup

Servings: 6

INGREDIENTS

1 can (28 ounces) petite diced tomatoes

1 medium onion, chopped

4 garlic cloves, sliced

1 teaspoon salt

1 teaspoon freshly ground pepper

1 teaspoon dried oregano

1 pound Italian turkey sausage, thinly sliced

3 ounces turkey pepperoni, diced

1 green bell pepper, diced

½ cup dry ditalini, pasta

½ cup mozzarella cheese, shredded

DIRECTIONS

1. Place all ingredients, except mozzarella cheese, into the pressure cooker; secure lid.
2. Press fish function, add 3 minutes; press start.
3. When cook time is complete, and pressure is fully vented, open lid.
4. Divide soup between bowls, top with cheese and serve.

TIP

Serve with a piece of garlic bread on the side.

NUTRITION FACTS

Serving Size:
1/6 of a recipe.

Amount Per Serving	% Daily Value
Calories: 451	23%
Calories from Fat: 301	45%
Total Fat: 32g	49%
Saturated Fat: 13g	65%
Cholesterol: 114mg	38%
Sodium: 1245mg	50%
Total Carbohydrates: 11g	4%
Fiber: 1g	4%
Sugars: 1g	
Protein: 25g	45%
Vitamin A:	0%
Vitamin C:	5%
Calcium:	0%
Iron:	16%

Potato Leek Soup

Servings: 6

INGREDIENTS

2 cups leeks (white part only) sliced

1 cup sweet onion, sliced

2 cups Yukon gold potatoes, peeled and diced

3 cups chicken stock

½ teaspoon salt

½ teaspoon freshly ground pepper

½ cup sour cream

1 teaspoon fresh chives, chopped

DIRECTIONS

1. Place all ingredients, except sour cream and chives, into the pressure cooker; secure lid.

2. Press rice function, minus 2 minutes; press start.

3. When cook time is complete, and pressure is fully vented, open lid.

4. Purée the soup using an immersion blender until desired consistency.

5. Serve topped with sour cream and chives.

TIP

This soup is even more delicious served cold.

NUTRITION FACTS

Serving Size:
1/6 of a recipe.

Amount Per Serving	% Daily Value
Calories: 300	30%
Calories from Fat: 53	8%
Total Fat: 6g	9%
Saturated Fat: 3g	15%
Cholesterol: 15mg	5%
Sodium: 330mg	20%
Total Carbohydrates: 13g	4%
Fiber: 1g	4%
Sugars: 1g	
Protein: 6g	11%
Vitamin A:	4%
Vitamin C:	9%
Calcium:	2%
Iron:	1%

Rich Beef Stock

Servings: 8

INGREDIENTS

4 pounds beef rib bones

1 cup red wine

1 tablespoon extra-virgin olive oil

5 cups water

1 tablespoon sea salt

2 celery stalks

1 teaspoon freshly ground pepper

1 carrot, peeled

1 medium sweet onion, quartered

2 sprigs fresh thyme

4 ounces button mushrooms

2 tablespoons tomato paste

5 garlic cloves

DIRECTIONS

1. Preheat oven to 350 degrees.
2. Place rib bones into an oven-safe skillet.
3. Add the oil, salt and pepper to the skillet; toss.
4. Add onions, mushrooms and garlic to the skillet; toss again.
5. Place skillet in the oven and roast for 1 hour.
6. Transfer the skillet contents to the pressure cooker.
7. Add wine to deglaze the skillet; scrape up all the little bits from the bottom of the skillet and transfer the skillet contents to the pressure cooker.
8. Add remaining ingredients to the pressure cooker; secure lid.
9. Press beans function, add 5 minutes; press start.
10. When cook time is complete, and pressure is fully vented, open lid.
11. Strain the stock through a fine sieve into a container with a lid.
12. Cover and refrigerate for 3 hours.
13. Remove hardened fat from the top of the stock before using.
14. Stock will keep refrigerated for up to one week or frozen for up to 6 months.

NUTRITION FACTS

Serving Size:
1/8 of a recipe.

Amount Per Serving	% Daily Value
Calories: 158	20%
Calories from Fat: 297	45%
Total Fat: 36g	55%
Saturated Fat: 11g	55%
Cholesterol: 293mg	98%
Sodium: 108mg	10%
Total Carbohydrates: 16g	5%
Fiber: 4g	16%
Sugars: 6g	
Protein: 110g	200%
Vitamin A:	2%
Vitamin C:	33%
Calcium:	9%
Iron:	54%

Rich Chicken Stock

Servings: 8

INGREDIENTS

2 pounds whole chicken wings, raw

3 garlic cloves

1 tablespoon extra-virgin olive oil

1 cup white wine

1 tablespoon sea salt

3 cups water

1 teaspoon black pepper

2 celery stalks, cut into 2-inch pieces

1 teaspoon poultry seasoning

1 teaspoon turmeric powder

1 leek (white part only) split

2 sprigs fresh thyme

1 parsnip, peeled, cut into 1-inch pieces

DIRECTIONS

1. Preheat oven to 350 degrees.
2. Place chicken wings into an oven-safe skillet.
3. 3. Add the oil, salt, pepper and poultry seasoning to the skillet; toss.
4. Add leek, parsnip and garlic to skillet; toss again.
5. Placed skillet in the oven and roast for 1 hour.
6. Transfer the skillet contents to the pressure cooker.
7. Add wine to deglaze the skillet; scrape up all the little bits from the bottom of the skillet and transfer the skillet contents to the pressure cooker.
8. Add remaining ingredients to the pressure cooker; secure lid.
9. Press bake function; press start.
10. When cook time is complete, and pressure is fully vented, open lid.
11. Strain the stock through a fine sieve into a container with a lid.
12. Cover and refrigerate for 3 hours.
13. Remove hardened fat from the top of the stock before using.
14. Stock will keep refrigerated for up to one week or frozen for up to 6 months.

NUTRITION FACTS

Serving Size:
1/8 of a recipe.

Amount Per Serving	% Daily Value
Calories: 120	7%
Calories from Fat: 30	4%
Calories: 108	5%
Calories from Fat: 30	4%
Cholesterol: 0mg	0%
Sodium: 79mg	5%
Total Carbohydrates: 16g	5%
Fiber: 4g	16%
Sugars: 0g	
Protein: 2g	4%
Vitamin A:	0%
Vitamin C:	30%
Calcium:	8%
Iron:	2%

Split Pea Soup

Servings: 6

INGREDIENTS

1 package (16 ounces) split peas with seasoning packet

2 cups pork shoulder, diced

3 carrots, peeled and sliced

½ cup onion, diced

2 stalks of celery, sliced

1 bay leaf

2 garlic cloves, minced

2 tablespoons parsley, chopped

1 teaspoon salt

½ teaspoon freshly ground pepper

1 teaspoon vinegar

6 cups of water

DIRECTIONS

1. Place all ingredients into the pressure cooker; secure lid.
2. Press rice function, minus 2 minutes; press start.
3. When cook time is complete, and pressure is fully vented, open lid.
4. Remove bay leaf and serve.

NUTRITION FACTS

Serving Size:
1/6 of a recipe.

Amount Per Serving	% Daily Value
Calories: 500	45%
Calories from Fat: 0	0%
Total Fat: 38g	0%
Saturated Fat: 73g	0%
Cholesterol: 0mg	0%
Sodium: 393mg	16%
Total Carbohydrates: 0g	0%
Fiber: 0g	0%
Sugars: 0g	
Protein: 0g	0%
Vitamin A:	0%
Vitamin C:	0%
Calcium:	0%
Iron:	0%

Shrimp Bisque

Servings: 8

INGREDIENTS

2 pounds large shrimp, with shells

1 leek (white part only) sliced

2 tablespoons extra-virgin olive oil

1 garlic clove, sliced

1 teaspoon salt

1 small potato, peeled and halved

1 teaspoon freshly ground pepper

1 tablespoon tomato paste

1 teaspoon sweet paprika

3 cups chicken stock

1 cup white wine

1 sprig tarragon

1 carrot, peeled and chopped

2 teaspoons sherry

1 celery stalk, chopped

1 cup heavy cream

DIRECTIONS

1. Dry shrimp using paper towels.
2. Preheat oil in a sauté pan over medium-high heat.
3. Add the shrimp to the pan and cook for 3 minutes on each side.
4. Season the shrimp with salt, pepper, and paprika, then transfer them to the pressure cooker.
5. Add wine to the pan; scrape up all the little bits from the bottom of the pan, then transfer the pan contents to the pressure cooker.
6. Add remaining ingredients, except heavy cream, to the pressure cooker; secure lid.
7. Turn pressure cooker on and set timer for 6 minutes.
8. When cooking is complete, remove tarragon sprig.
9. Using an immersion blender, puree the soup while adding the cream; puree until desired consistency before serving.

NUTRITION FACTS

Serving Size:
1/8 of a recipe.

Amount Per Serving	% Daily Value
Calories: 350	18%
Calories from Fat: 276	41%
Total Fat: 32g	49%
Saturated Fat: 13g	65%
Cholesterol: 381mg	127%
Sodium: 1000mg	50%
Total Carbohydrates: 9g	3%
Fiber: 0g	0%
Sugars: 3g	
Protein: 30g	55%
Vitamin A:	27%
Vitamin C:	1%
Calcium:	3%
Iron:	3%

Tomato Florentine Soup

Servings: 8

INGREDIENTS

2 pounds grape tomatoes

6 cups of chicken stock

1 carrot, peeled and sliced

1 medium onion, chopped

3 garlic cloves, sliced

1 teaspoon salt

1 teaspoon freshly ground pepper

1 cup dry pasta

1 cup baby spinach leaves

5 basil leaves, torn

DIRECTIONS

1. Place all ingredients, except basil, into the pressure cooker; secure lid.
2. Press fish function, add 3 minutes; press start.
3. When cook time is complete, and pressure is fully vented, open lid.
4. Top with basil leaves and serve.

TIP

Garnish with a touch of pesto.

NUTRITION FACTS

Serving Size:
1/8 of a recipe.

Amount Per Serving	% Daily Value
Calories: 217	11%
Calories from Fat: 20	3%
Total Fat: 3g	5%
Saturated Fat: 0g	0%
Cholesterol: 0mg	0%
Sodium: 800mg	35%
Total Carbohydrates: 32g	11%
Fiber: 3g	12%
Sugars: 1g	
Protein: 12g	22%
Vitamin A:	30%
Vitamin C:	65%
Calcium:	0%
Iron:	8%

Swiss Chard White Bean Stew

Servings: 4

INGREDIENTS

1 bunch Swiss chard washed and cut into 1-inch pieces.

1 medium sweet onion, diced

3 garlic cloves, sliced

1 pound red bliss potatoes, washed and diced

1 cup white beans, cooked

2 sprigs fresh thyme

1 cup vegetable stock

1 teaspoon salt

½ teaspoon freshly ground pepper

DIRECTIONS

1. Place all ingredients into the pressure cooker; secure lid.
2. Press rice function, minus 2 minutes; press start.
3. When cook time is complete, and pressure is fully vented, open lid.
4. Remove and discard the thyme sprig and serve.

TIP

Serve this delicious stew topped with grated Parmesan cheese and a slice of crusty bread.

NUTRITION FACTS

Serving Size:
1/4 of a recipe.

Amount Per Serving	% Daily Value
Calories: 134	7%
Calories from Fat: 3	0%
Total Fat: 0g	0%
Saturated Fat: 0g	0%
Cholesterol: 0mg	0%
Sodium: 930mg	39%
Total Carbohydrates: 25g	8%
Fiber: 4g	16%
Sugars: 3g	
Protein: 5g	9%
Vitamin A:	3%
Vitamin C:	19%
Calcium:	4%
Iron:	7%

DESSERTS

Caramel Apple Cake

Servings: 8

INGREDIENTS

2 Granny Smith apples, peeled cored and sliced
¼ cup unsalted butter
¼ cup brown sugar
1 spice cake mix (batter prepared to box instructions)
Nonstick spray

DIRECTIONS

1. Select the brown/sauté function; add the butter and brown sugar.
2. Stir until melted, add the apples and cook for 3 minutes.
3. Spray only the sides of the insert with nonstick spray.
4. Pour the cake batter into the pressure cooker, secure lid.
5. When cook time is complete, and pressure is fully released, invert onto cake stand while still warm.

TIP

Serve warm or cold with extra caramel sauce and whipped cream.

NUTRITION FACTS

Serving Size:
1/8 of a recipe.

Amount Per Serving	% Daily Value
Calories: 73	4%
Calories from Fat: 50	8%
Total Fat: 6g	9%
Saturated Fat: 0g	0%
Cholesterol: 15mg	5%
Sodium: 45mg	2%
Total Carbohydrates: 6g	2%
Fiber: 0g	0%
Sugars: 6g	
Protein: 0g	0%
Vitamin A:	4%
Vitamin C:	0%
Calcium:	0%
Iron:	0%

Chocolate Caramel Bread Pudding

Servings: 6

INGREDIENTS

6 ounces caramel chips

4 large eggs, beaten

1 ½ cups heavy cream

½ cup brown sugar

1 teaspoon vanilla extract

1 cup dark chocolate chips

1 loaf challah bread, cubed and toasted

Nonstick spray

DIRECTIONS

1. Add ingredients to a bowl; mix well.
2. Apply nonstick spray to the pressure cooker.
3. Transfer bowl contents to the pressure cooker; secure lid.
4. Press grains function, and then press start.
5. When cook time is complete, and pressure is fully vented, open lid.
6. Serve hot or cold

NUTRITION FACTS

Serving Size:
1/6 of a recipe.

Amount Per Serving	% Daily Value
Calories: 531	27%
Calories from Fat: 248	37%
Total Fat: 29g	45%
Saturated Fat: 13g	65%
Cholesterol: 176mg	59%
Sodium: 529mg	22%
Total Carbohydrates: 61g	20%
Fiber: 3g	12%
Sugars: 22g	
Protein: 9g	16%
Vitamin A:	19%
Vitamin C:	0%
Calcium:	7%
Iron:	20%

Coconut Soup

Servings: 4

INGREDIENTS

2 cans (13.5 ounces each) light coconut milk
¼ cup small pearl tapioca
¼ cup sugar
¼ cup sweetened coconut, shredded
1 teaspoon coconut extract

DIRECTIONS

1. Place coconut milk, tapioca and sugar into the pressure cooker; secure lid.
2. Press vegetable function plus 1 minute, press start.
3. When cook time is completed, and pressure has been fully vented, open lid.
4. Stir in remaining ingredients; let cool.
5. Pour soup into glasses and serve chilled.

NUTRITION FACTS

Serving Size:
1/4 of a recipe.

Amount Per Serving	% Daily Value
Calories: 80	4%
Calories from Fat: 0	0%
Total Fat: 0g	0%
Saturated Fat: 0g	0%
Cholesterol: 0mg	0%
Sodium: 0mg	0%
Total Carbohydrates: 21g	7%
Fiber: 0g	0%
Sugars: 12g	
Protein: 0g	0%
Vitamin A:	0%
Vitamin C:	0%
Calcium:	0%
Iron:	0%

Creamy Quinoa Pudding

Servings: 4

INGREDIENTS

1 cup quinoa, rinsed

1 cup water

1 ½ cups rice milk

2 tablespoons agave syrup

pinch of salt

1 vanilla bean, split

¼ cup dried cranberries

DIRECTIONS

1. Place all ingredients into the pressure cooker; secure lid.
2. Press rice function, press start.
3. When cook time is complete and the pressure has been fully vented, open lid.
4. Remove vanilla bean and scrape the inside of the bean into the pudding; stir.
5. Serve immediately.

NUTRITION FACTS

Serving Size:
1/4 of a recipe.

Amount Per Serving	% Daily Value
Calories: 73	4%
Calories from Fat: 17	3%
Total Fat: 2g	3%
Saturated Fat: 1g	5%
Cholesterol: 8mg	3%
Sodium: 84mg	4%
Total Carbohydrates: 11g	4%
Fiber: 0g	0%
Sugars: 10g	
Protein: 3g	5%
Vitamin A:	4%
Vitamin C:	2%
Calcium:	11%
Iron:	0%

Mint Chocolate Cheesecake

Servings: 4

INGREDIENTS

14 thin mint chocolate cookies

2 tablespoons unsalted butter

½ cup heavy cream

1 cup semi-sweet chocolate morsels

½ teaspoon mint extracts

1 teaspoon mint extract

1 ½ cups semi-sweet chocolate morsels

2 packages (8 ounces each) cream cheese

½ cup sugar

1 tablespoon all-purpose flour

2 large eggs

1 teaspoon vanilla extract

DIRECTIONS

1. Preheat oven to 350 degrees; place sheet of parchment paper over the base of a 7 inch spring form pan, secure ring around the pan then apply nonstick spray to the inside of the pan.

2. Place cookies and butter into a food processor and process until smooth; press the mixture into the base of the spring form pan and bake for 10 minutes.

3. In a microwave-safe bowl, microwave chocolate morsels for the filling at 50% power for 1 minute; stir and microwave for an additional 30 seconds.

4. In a food processor, combine the cream cheese and sugar; process until smooth then add remaining filling ingredients to the food processor; mix well then add the melted chocolate to the food processor and process until smooth.

5. Pour the filling into the spring form pan and wrap it tightly in aluminum foil.

6. Pour 1 cup of water into the pressure cooker, then place the pan into the pressure cooker; secure lid.

7. Press bean function, press start.

8. When cook time is complete, and pressure is fully vented, open lid.

9. Remove pan from the pressure cooker and let cool at room temperature.

10. To make fudge topping, in a sauce pan over medium heat, bring cream to a boil; remove from heat, add chocolate to the saucepan. Stir until smooth, then add mint extract.

11. Pour fudge topping over the cheesecake, cover in plastic wrap and refrigerate for 2 hours before serving.

NUTRITION FACTS

Serving Size:
1/4 of a recipe.

Amount Per Serving	% Daily Value
Calories: 456	23%
Calories from Fat: 222	33%
Total Fat: 26g	40%
Saturated Fat: 8g	40%
Cholesterol: 127mg	42%
Sodium: 129mg	5%
Total Carbohydrates: 54g	18%
Fiber: 1g	4%
Sugars: 36g	
Protein: 4g	7%
Vitamin A:	14%
Vitamin C:	0%
Calcium:	1%
Iron:	4%

Easy Crème Caramel

Servings: 6

INGREDIENTS

½ cup sugar

1 ½ cups water, divided

6 custard cups, 4-ounce capacity

1 can (14 ounce) sweetened condensed milk

1 can (12 ounce) evaporated milk

2 large eggs, beaten

1 teaspoon vanilla extract

1 teaspoon orange zest

DIRECTIONS

1. Preheat stove top on high.
2. In a nonstick pan, combine sugar and ½ cup water; stir until sugar is dissolved.
3. Reduce heat to medium and let sugar mixture cook for several minutes; do not stir.
4. When water evaporates and the sugar turns a caramel color, remove from heat then pour into custard cups; let rest for 10 minutes.
5. Pour remaining water into pressure cooker.
6. In a bowl, combine remaining ingredients, stir, and then pour into custard cups.
7. Cover each cup with aluminum foil and stack cups inside pressure cooker; secure lid.
8. Press vegetable function, add 1 minute; press start.
9. When cook time is complete, and pressure has fully vented, open lid.
10. Remove cups and chill until ready to serve.

NUTRITION FACTS

Serving Size:
1/6 of a recipe.

Amount Per Serving	% Daily Value
Calories: 76	4%
Calories from Fat: 9	1%
Total Fat: 1g	2%
Saturated Fat: 0g	0%
Cholesterol: 48mg	16%
Sodium: 14mg	1%
Total Carbohydrates: 16g	5%
Fiber: 0g	0%
Sugars: 16g	
Protein: 1g	2%
Vitamin A:	1%
Vitamin C:	0%
Calcium:	0%
Iron:	2%

Orange Pots de Crème

Servings: 4

INGREDIENTS

1 large egg

4 eggs yolks

¼ cup sugar

½ cup orange juice

1 cup heavy cream

1 teaspoon lemon juice

1 teaspoon lemon zest

1 cup water

DIRECTIONS

1. In a large bowl, combine egg, yolks and sugar; beat for 30 seconds using a fork.
2. Add heavy cream, juices and zest to the bowl; whisk until sugar is dissolved.
3. Strain the custard through a sieve.
4. Apply nonstick spray to four ½-cup ramekins; set aside.
5. Divide custard between four ½-cup ramekins.
6. Wrap each ramekin in aluminum foil.
7. Pour water into the pressure cooker.
8. Place ramekins inside the pressure cooker; secure lid.
9. Press fish function; then press start.
10. When cook time is complete, and pressure is fully vented, open lid.
11. Remove the foil and chill for 30 minutes before serving.

NUTRITION FACTS

Serving Size:
1/4 of a recipe.

Amount Per Serving	% Daily Value
Calories: 317	16%
Calories from Fat: 233	35%
Total Fat: 28g	43%
Saturated Fat: 13g	65%
Cholesterol: 259mg	86%
Sodium: 74mg	3%
Total Carbohydrates: 16g	5%
Fiber: 0g	0%
Sugars: 15g	
Protein: 5g	9%
Vitamin A:	21%
Vitamin C:	16%
Calcium:	2%
Iron:	3%

Healthy Hazelnut Rice Pudding

Servings: 6

INGREDIENTS

4 cups brown rice, cooked

4 cups milk

1/8 teaspoon salt

½ cup sugar

1 stick cinnamon

½ cup golden raisins

1 tablespoon hazelnut liqueur

¼ cup raisins

DIRECTIONS

1. Place all ingredients into the pressure cooker; secure lid.
2. Press rice function then start.
3. When cook time is complete, and pressure is fully vented, open lid.
4. Stir in raisins, serve hot or cold.

NUTRITION FACTS

Serving Size:
1/6 of a recipe.

Amount Per Serving	% Daily Value
Calories: 674	34%
Calories from Fat: 78	12%
Total Fat: 9g	14%
Saturated Fat: 2g	10%
Cholesterol: 13mg	4%
Sodium: 138mg	6%
Total Carbohydrates: 139g	46%
Fiber: 9g	36%
Sugars: 39g	
Protein: 14g	25%
Vitamin A:	7%
Vitamin C:	3%
Calcium:	21%
Iron:	3%

Poached Pears

Servings: 4

INGREDIENTS

1 bottle (750ml) port wine

4 Bartlett pears

3 sprigs rosemary

½ teaspoon whole peppercorns

DIRECTIONS

1. Pour the wine into the pressure cooker.
2. Using a melon baller, core the bottom of each pear.
3. Cut off the bottom of each pear so they sit flat.
4. Place the pears into the pressure cooker.
5. Add the rosemary and peppercorns to the pressure cooker; secure lid.
6. Press vegetable function plus 5 minutes, press start.
7. When cook time is complete, and pressure is fully vented, open lid.
8. Transfer the pears to a platter.
9. To reduce liquid in the pressure cooker, press brown/sauté function and cook with lid off until liquid turns into syrup.
10. Top pears with syrup and serve.

TIP

Serve poached pears topped with your favorite ice cream.

NUTRITION FACTS

Serving Size:
1/4 of a recipe.

Amount Per Serving	% Daily Value
Calories: 99	5%
Calories from Fat: 0	0%
Total Fat: 1g	2%
Saturated Fat: 0g	0%
Cholesterol: 0mg	0%
Sodium: 32mg	1%
Total Carbohydrates: 4g	1%
Fiber: 4g	16%
Sugars: 0g	
Protein: 1g	2%
Vitamin A:	0%
Vitamin C:	10%
Calcium:	2%
Iron:	2%

Orange Upside Down Cake

Servings: 6

INGREDIENTS

2 tablespoons unsalted butter

1 teaspoon ground cinnamon

2 tablespoons brown sugar

½ teaspoon allspice

1 teaspoon maple syrup

½ cup safflower oil

1 large orange, sliced into thin rings

1 cup carrots, shredded

1 ½ cups unbleached all-purpose flour

1 cup applesauce

1 cup sugar

½ cup raisins

1 teaspoon baking powder

1 teaspoon vanilla extract

1 teaspoon baking soda

¼ cup chopped pecans (optional)

DIRECTIONS

1. Place butter into the pressure cooker.
2. Press brown/sauté function and let butter melt with the lid off.
3. Add brown sugar and syrup to the pressure cooker; stir until smooth.
4. Turn off pressure cooker, then top sugar mixture with layers of orange rings.
5. In a large bowl, combine flour, sugar, baking powder, baking soda, cinnamon and allspice; mix well.
6. In a separate bowl, combine oil, carrots, applesauce and vanilla; mix well
7. Add carrot mixture to the flour mixture and mix using a spatula; add remaining ingredients and mix well.
8. Apply nonstick spray to the pressure cooker.
9. Pour batter evenly into the pressure cooker over the orange slices; secure id.
10. Press bake function, then press start.
11. When cook time is complete, and pressure is fully vented, open lid.
12. Remove lid and let the cake rest for 20 minutes inside the pressure cooker.
13. Invert the cake onto a cake stand and serve.

NUTRITION FACTS

Serving Size:
1/6 of a recipe.

Amount Per Serving	% Daily Value
Calories: 530	26%
Calories from Fat: 217	33%
Total Fat: 25g	38%
Saturated Fat: 2g	10%
Cholesterol: 10mg	3%
Sodium: 291mg	12%
Total Carbohydrates: 77g	26%
Fiber: 2g	8%
Sugars: 52g	
Protein: 1g	2%
Vitamin A:	3%
Vitamin C:	0%
Calcium:	1%
Iron:	9%

Hot Fudge Cake

Servings: 8

INGREDIENTS

1 box (18.25 ounces) chocolate fudge cake mix

1 cup heavy cream

3 large eggs

½ cup unsalted butter

2 cups water

DIRECTIONS

1. Apply a nonstick spray to a 2-quart stainless steel bowl or baking insert.

2. Place all ingredients, except water, into a food processor; mix until smooth, then transfer to the stainless steel bowl.

3. Pour water into the pressure cooker and place the bowl in the water; secure lid.

4. Press bake function; press start.

5. When cook time is complete, and pressure is fully vented, open lid.

6. Invert onto a cake stand and serve.

NUTRITION FACTS

Serving Size:
1/8 of a recipe.

Amount Per Serving	% Daily Value
Calories: 218	11%
Calories from Fat: 210	31%
Total Fat: 24g	37%
Saturated Fat: 6g	30%
Cholesterol: 124mg	41%
Sodium: 116mg	5%
Total Carbohydrates: 0g	0%
Fiber: 0g	0%
Sugars: 0g	
Protein: 2g	4%
Vitamin A:	18%
Vitamin C:	0%
Calcium:	1%
Iron:	1%

Lemon Curd

Servings: 4

INGREDIENTS

1 ¼ cups sugar

2 tablespoons lemon zest

½ cup bottled lemon juice

⅓ cup unsalted butter, cut into small pieces

4 egg yolks

3 large eggs

1 cup water

DIRECTIONS

1. Process the sugar in a blender until very fine, then transfer it to a 2 quart bowl.
2. Add remaining ingredients, except water, to the bowl; beat using a whisk.
3. Cover the bowl tightly in aluminum foil.
4. Pour water in the pressure cooker.
5. Place the bowl into the pressure cooker; secure lid.
6. Press rice function, add 1 minute and press start.
7. When cook time is complete, and pressure is fully vented, open lid.
8. Carefully remove the foil, then whisk the ingredients well.
9. Refrigerate for 1 hour before serving.

NUTRITION FACTS

Serving Size:
1/4 of a recipe.

Amount Per Serving	% Daily Value
Calories: 440	22%
Calories from Fat: 180	27%
Total Fat: 20g	31%
Saturated Fat: 2g	10%
Cholesterol: 291mg	97%
Sodium: 196mg	8%
Total Carbohydrates: 61g	20%
Fiber: 0g	0%
Sugars: 60g	
Protein: 7g	13%
Vitamin A:	18%
Vitamin C:	0%
Calcium:	2%
Iron:	5%

Key Lime Cheesecake

Servings: 6

INGREDIENTS

10 vanilla wafers

2 tablespoons unsalted butter

¼ cup Macadamia nuts

3 large eggs

3 packages (8 ounces each) cream cheese

1 can (14 ounces) sweetened condensed milk

1 tablespoon all-purpose flour

⅓ cup key lime juice

1 teaspoon lime zest

1 teaspoon butter nut extract

2 drops green food coloring (optional)

DIRECTIONS

1. Preheat oven to 350 degrees; place sheet of parchment paper over the base of a 7-inch spring form pan, secure ring around the pan then apply non-stick spray to the inside of the pan.

2. Place wafers, butter, and nuts into a food processor and process until smooth; press the mixture into the base of the spring form pan and bake for 10 minutes.

3. Place cream cheese and milk into the food processor; processor for 1 minute or until very smooth; while processing, add eggs (one at a time) through the feed tube then continue to process for 30 seconds.

4. Add remaining ingredients, then process an additional 30 seconds.

5. Pour filling into the baked crust, then wrap the entire spring-form pan in aluminum foil.

6. Pour 1 cup of water into the pressure cooker then place the pan into the pressure cooker; secure lid.

7. Press beans function, press start.

8. When cook time is complete, and pressure is fully vented, open lid.

9. Let cool at room temperature for 30 minutes.

10. Refrigerate the covered cheesecake for 2 hours before serving.

NUTRITION FACTS

Serving Size:
1/6 of a recipe.

Amount Per Serving	% Daily Value
Calories: 131	7%
Calories from Fat: 86	13%
Total Fat: 10g	15%
Saturated Fat: 1g	5%
Cholesterol: 83mg	28%
Sodium: 73mg	3%
Total Carbohydrates: 8g	3%
Fiber: 0g	0%
Sugars: 0g	
Protein: 2g	4%
Vitamin A:	5%
Vitamin C:	0%
Calcium:	1%
Iron:	3%

BEEF, PORK, AND LAMB

Braised Beef Short Ribs

Servings: 4

INGREDIENTS

4 beef short ribs

4 garlic cloves

1 cup beef stock

1 shallot, halved

1 teaspoon salt

2 sprigs fresh thyme

½ teaspoon freshly ground pepper

1 tablespoon Worcestershire sauce

1 leek (white part only) split

¼ cup red wine

2 carrots, peeled and cut into 2-inch slices

1 teaspoon soy sauce

2 celery stalks, sliced

1 tablespoon tomato paste

DIRECTIONS

1. Place all ingredients, except wine and tomato paste, into the pressure cooker; secure lid.
2. Press beans function; press start.
3. Add the wine and tomato paste to the pressure cooker; stir and secure the lid.
4. Press grain function, add 5 minutes; press start.
5. When cook time is complete, and pressure is fully vented, open lid.
6. Strain the pressure cooker contents through a sieve into a container; reserve the vegetables in a bowl.
7. Refrigerate stock for 30 minutes.
8. Place short ribs back into the pressure cooker.
9. Turn pressure cooker on to keep warm.
10. Using a blender, puree the vegetables until smooth; then place them back into the pressure cooker.
11. Remove the stock from the refrigerator, discard the hardened fat and pour stock back into the pressure cooker.
12. Stir until heated; then serve.

NUTRITION FACTS

Serving Size:
1/4 of a recipe.

Amount Per Serving	% Daily Value
Calories: 46	2%
Calories from Fat: 0	0%
Total Fat: 0g	0%
Saturated Fat: 0g	0%
Cholesterol: 0mg	0%
Sodium: 12mg	1%
Total Carbohydrates: 10g	3%
Fiber: 2g	8%
Sugars: 0g	
Protein: 1g	2%
Vitamin A:	10%
Vitamin C:	20%
Calcium:	0%
Iron:	1%

Corned Beef Rueben

Servings: 4

INGREDIENTS

1 (2 pound) corned beef brisket, sliced ½-inch thick

1 medium onion, quartered

1 carrot, peeled

½ cup water

1 teaspoon mustard seeds

1 bay leaf

8 slices rye bread, toasted

1 cup sauerkraut, drained

4 Swiss cheese, slices

2 tablespoons Thousand Island dressing

DIRECTIONS

1. Place all ingredients, except bread, sauerkraut, cheese and dressing, into the pressure cooker; secure lid.

2. Press beans function, add 5 minutes; press start.

3. Divide the sauerkraut between 4 bread slices then top each slice with 1 slice of cheese and ½ tablespoon of Thousand Island dressing.

4. When cook time is complete, and pressure is fully vented, open lid.

5. Divide corned beef between the prepared slices and top each with another slice of bread.

6. Serve immediately.

NUTRITION FACTS

Serving Size:
1/4 of a recipe.

Amount Per Serving	% Daily Value
Calories: 1116	56%
Calories from Fat: 653	98%
Total Fat: 72g	111%
Saturated Fat: 27g	135%
Cholesterol: 267mg	89%
Sodium: 946mg	39%
Total Carbohydrates: 30g	10%
Fiber: 5g	20%
Sugars: 0g	
Protein: 80g	145%
Vitamin A:	0%
Vitamin C:	9%
Calcium:	4%
Iron:	42%

Italian Pot Roast

Servings: 4

INGREDIENTS

2 tablespoons extra-virgin olive oil

1 (4 pound) chuck roast

1 teaspoon salt

½ teaspoon freshly ground pepper

¼ cup dry red wine

1 cup beef stock

3 garlic cloves, sliced

1 bell pepper, diced

1 teaspoon garlic powder

1 teaspoon Italian herb, seasoning

1 bay leaf

1 bottle (28 ounces) pasta sauce

1 medium onion, sliced

Pasta, or polenta, cooked

DIRECTIONS

1. Press browning function, add oil and preheat.
2. Season the roast with salt and pepper.
3. Add the roast to the skillet then sear for 3 minutes on each side.
4. Transfer the roast to a platter and cover.
5. Drain fat from the pressure cooker.
6. Add wine and stock to deglaze the pressure cooker; scrape up all the little bits from the bottom.
7. Add onions, garlic, bell peppers, garlic powder, Italian seasoning and bay leaf to the pressure cooker; secure lid.
8. Press beans function, add 20 minutes; press start.
9. When cook time is complete, and pressure is fully vented, open lid.
10. Discard the bay leaf then add the pasta sauce to the pressure cooker; secure lid.
11. Press fish function, add 1 minute; press start.
12. When cooking is complete, and pressure is fully vented, open lid.
13. Serve over your favorite pasta or polenta.

NUTRITION FACTS

Serving Size:
1/4 of a recipe.

Amount Per Serving	% Daily Value
Calories: 117	6%
Calories from Fat: 77	12%
Total Fat: 9g	14%
Saturated Fat: 2g	10%
Cholesterol: 18mg	6%
Sodium: 733mg	31%
Total Carbohydrates: 3g	1%
Fiber: 0g	0%
Sugars: 0g	
Protein: 7g	13%
Vitamin A:	0%
Vitamin C:	5%
Calcium:	0%
Iron:	4%

Meatballs for Spaghetti

Servings: 6

INGREDIENTS

1 ½ cups fresh breadcrumbs

4 tablespoons extra-virgin olive oil

4 cups beef stock, divided

4 tablespoons tomato paste

1 pound ground chuck

2 cans (28 ounces each) Italian tomatoes

½ pound ground pork

3 garlic cloves, minced

1 small onion, minced

1 small onion, minced

¾ cup Romano cheese, grated

1 teaspoon dry, oregano

1 teaspoon salt

1 teaspoon dried, basil

½ teaspoon freshly ground, pepper

2 large eggs, beaten

DIRECTIONS

1. In a bowl, soak the breadcrumbs in 2 cups of beef stock.
2. Pour remaining stock into the pressure cooker.
3. Add remaining ingredients to the breadcrumbs; mix then form into 2-inch meatballs.
4. Place meatballs into the pressure cooker; secure lid.
5. Press grain function, add 5 minutes; press start.
6. When cook time is complete, and pressure is fully vented, open lid.
7. Transfer meatballs to a platter then pour the stock into a separate bowl and skim off the fat.
8. Dissolve tomato paste in the strained stock then pour it into the pressure cooker.
9. Add remaining ingredients and meatballs to the pressure cooker; secure lid.
10. Press grain function; press start.
11. When cook time is complete, and pressure is fully vented, open lid.
12. Serve over spaghetti.

NUTRITION FACTS

Serving Size:
1/6 of a recipe.

Amount Per Serving	% Daily Value
Calories: 397	20%
Calories from Fat: 244	37%
Total Fat: 29g	45%
Saturated Fat: 10g	50%
Cholesterol: 137mg	46%
Sodium: 1038mg	43%
Total Carbohydrates: 4g	1%
Fiber: 1g	4%
Sugars: 3g	
Protein: 26g	47%
Vitamin A:	4%
Vitamin C:	10%
Calcium:	13%
Iron:	12%

Moroccan Lamb Shanks

Servings: 4

INGREDIENTS

2 tablespoons extra-virgin olive oil

4 (1 pound each) lamb shanks

½ teaspoon salt

½ teaspoon freshly ground pepper

½ cup dry red wine

½ cup chicken stock

2 tablespoons tomato paste

½ cup carrot, diced

1 shallot, minced

3 garlic cloves, minced

½ teaspoon cumin seeds

½ teaspoon pumpkin pie spice

1 can (16.5 ounces) petite diced tomatoes

2 tablespoons fresh cilantro, chopped

DIRECTIONS

1. Press browning function, add oil and preheat
2. Season lamb shanks with salt and pepper.
3. Add the lamb to the pressure cooker and sear each shank on all sides until browned.
4. Transfer the lamb shanks to a platter, cover.
5. Drain fat from the pressure cooker.
6. Add red wine to deglaze the pressure cooker; scrape up all the little bits from the bottom.
7. Add remaining ingredients, except cilantro, to the pressure cooker; secure lid.
8. Press beans function, add 20 minutes; press start.
9. When cook time is complete, and pressure is fully vented, open lid.
10. Top with cilantro and serve.

NUTRITION FACTS

Serving Size:
1/4 of a recipe.

Amount Per Serving	% Daily Value
Calories: 71	4%
Calories from Fat: 61	9%
Total Fat: 7g	11%
Saturated Fat: 1g	5%
Cholesterol: 0mg	0%
Sodium: 404mg	17%
Total Carbohydrates: 1g	0%
Fiber: 0g	0%
Sugars: 1g	
Protein: 1g	2%
Vitamin A:	4%
Vitamin C:	3%
Calcium:	1%
Iron:	1%

Pork Chops l'Orange

Servings: 4

INGREDIENTS

4 bone-in pork chops, 1-inch thick

1 tablespoon extra-virgin olive oil

½ teaspoon salt

½ cup chicken stock

¼ cup brown sugar

1 teaspoon cider vinegar

1 teaspoon freshly grated ginger

½ teaspoon dry mustard

1 teaspoon dried marjoram

1 teaspoon orange zest

1 sprig fresh thyme

½ teaspoon black pepper

2 oranges, peeled and sectioned

DIRECTIONS

1. Press brown/sauté function and preheat pressure cooker.
2. Rub the pork chops with olive oil then season with salt.
3. Place pork chops into the pressure cooker and sear for 2 minutes on each side.
4. Add chicken stock to deglaze the pressure cooker; scrape up all the little bits from the bottom.
5. Add remaining ingredients to the pressure cooker; secure lid.
6. Press grain function, add 5 minutes; press start.
7. When cook time is complete, and pressure is fully vented, open lid.
8. Serve immediately.

NUTRITION FACTS

Serving Size:
1/4 of a recipe.

Amount Per Serving	% Daily Value
Calories: 296	15%
Calories from Fat: 126	19%
Total Fat: 12g	18%
Saturated Fat: 7g	35%
Cholesterol: 73mg	24%
Sodium: 447mg	19%
Total Carbohydrates: 12g	4%
Fiber: 0g	0%
Sugars: 12g	
Protein: 1g	2%
Vitamin A:	0%
Vitamin C:	0%
Calcium:	0%
Iron:	10%

Osso Buco

Servings: 4

INGREDIENTS

2 pounds meaty veal shanks

½ cup onion, diced

½ cup celery, deiced

½ cup parsnip, diced

2 garlic cloves, minced

1 teaspoon salt

½ teaspoon freshly ground pepper

½ cup vermouth

1 can (4.5 ounces) petite diced tomatoes

1 sprig thyme

1 teaspoon orange zest

1 cup beef stock

DIRECTIONS

1. Place all ingredients into the pressure cooker; secure lid.
2. Press beans function; press start.
3. Remove the thyme sprig then transfer the veal to a platter.
4. With the lid off, Press brown/sauté function to reduce the sauce.
5. Using a blender, puree the sauce.
6. Pour sauce over the veal and serve.

NUTRITION FACTS

Serving Size:
1/4 of a recipe.

Amount Per Serving	% Daily Value
Calories: 88	4%
Calories from Fat: 17	3%
Total Fat: 2g	3%
Saturated Fat: 1g	5%
Cholesterol: 18mg	6%
Sodium: 731mg	30%
Total Carbohydrates: 3g	1%
Fiber: 0g	0%
Sugars: 0g	
Protein: 7g	13%
Vitamin A:	0%
Vitamin C:	0%
Calcium:	0%
Iron:	3%

Stuffed Cabbage Rolls

Servings: 4

INGREDIENTS

½ pound ground chuck

½ pound ground pork

1 small onion, chopped

½ cup white rice, uncooked

½ teaspoon thyme leaves

1 teaspoon fresh dill, chopped

1 cup Swiss cheese, shredded

8 large cabbage leaves

Toothpicks

1 cup beef stock

1 can (15 ounces) tomato sauce

1 teaspoon sugar

1 teaspoon oregano

½ teaspoon garlic powder

1 tablespoon cider vinegar

DIRECTIONS

1. In a bowl, combine the meats, onions, rice, thyme, dill and cheese; mix well.
2. Place ⅓ cup of the meat mixture onto each cabbage leaf; fold in the sides then roll up.
3. Secure rolls with toothpicks then place them into the pressure cooker.
4. In a bowl, combine remaining ingredients then pour them into the pressure cooker; secure lid.
5. Press grains function, add 5 minutes; press start.
6. When cook time is complete, and pressure is fully vented, open lid.
7. Serve immediately.

NUTRITION FACTS

Serving Size:
1/4 of a recipe.

Amount Per Serving	% Daily Value
Calories: 282	14%
Calories from Fat: 138	21%
Total Fat: 15g	23%
Saturated Fat: 6g	30%
Cholesterol: 56mg	19%
Sodium: 170mg	7%
Total Carbohydrates: 19g	6%
Fiber: 1g	4%
Sugars: 2g	
Protein: 7g	13%
Vitamin A:	0%
Vitamin C:	5%
Calcium:	0%
Iron:	9%

Sweet and Sour Pork Chops

Servings: 4

INGREDIENTS

4 bone-in pork chops, 1-inch thick

1 tablespoon extra-virgin olive oil

½ teaspoon salt

½ cup chicken stock

¼ cup brown sugar

1 teaspoon cider vinegar

1 teaspoon freshly grated ginger

½ teaspoon dry mustard

1 teaspoon dried marjoram

¼ cup orange liquor

1 teaspoon orange zest

1 sprig fresh thyme

½ teaspoon black pepper

2 oranges, peeled and sectioned

DIRECTIONS

1. Preheat a large skillet over medium–high heat.
2. Rub the pork chops with olive oil then season with salt.
3. Place pork chops into the skillet and sear for 2 minutes on each side.
4. Transfer pork chops to the pressure cooker.
5. Add chicken stock to deglaze the skillet; scrape up all the little bits from the bottom of the skillet then transfer the skillet contents to the pressure cooker.
6. Add remaining ingredients to the pressure cooker; secure lid.
7. Press grain function, add 5 minutes; press start.
8. When cook time is complete, and pressure is fully vented, open lid.
9. Serve immediately.

NUTRITION FACTS

Serving Size:
1/4 of a recipe.

Amount Per Serving	% Daily Value
Calories: 299	15%
Calories from Fat: 126	19%
Total Fat: 12g	18%
Saturated Fat: 7g	35%
Cholesterol: 73mg	24%
Sodium: 447mg	19%
Total Carbohydrates: 13g	4%
Fiber: 0g	0%
Sugars: 12g	
Protein: 1g	2%
Vitamin A:	0%
Vitamin C:	6%
Calcium:	0%
Iron:	10%

Low Country Boil

Servings: 4

INGREDIENTS

5 cups water

1 tablespoon pickling spice

1 cup white wine

1 tablespoon crab seasoning

1 medium onion, quartered

6 red bliss potatoes

4 whole garlic cloves

1 pound spicy, smoked sausage

1 lemon, halved

2 ears of corn, cut in half

1 tablespoon kosher salt

2 pounds large shrimp, in the shell

1 teaspoon cayenne pepper

1 dozen little neck clams, cleaned and in the shell

1 celery stalk

DIRECTIONS

1. Place all ingredients, except corn, shrimp and clams into the pressure cooker; secure lid.
2. Press rice function, minus 2 minutes; press start.
3. When cook time is complete, and pressure is fully vented, open lid.
4. Add remaining ingredients to the pressure cooker; secure lid.
5. Press fish function; press start.
6. When cook time is complete, and pressure is fully vented, open lid.
7. Serve immediately.

TIP

Place the pressure cooker in the middle of the table, have bibs for all the guests and serve with drawn butter.

NUTRITION FACTS

Serving Size:
1/4 of a recipe.

Amount Per Serving	% Daily Value
Calories: 493	25%
Calories from Fat: 288	43%
Total Fat: 30g	46%
Saturated Fat: 0g	0%
Cholesterol: 371mg	124%
Sodium: 5026mg	209%
Total Carbohydrates: 11g	4%
Fiber: 0g	0%
Sugars: 5g	
Protein: 41g	75%
Vitamin A:	0%
Vitamin C:	5%
Calcium:	3%
Iron:	7%

Bangkok Baby Back Ribs

Servings: 2

INGREDIENTS

1 full slab baby back ribs
½ cup chicken stock
2 tablespoons fresh ginger, sliced
1 medium onion, quartered
2 garlic cloves
2 tablespoons sesame oil
2 tablespoons soy sauce
2 tablespoons rice wine vinegar
2 tablespoons brown sugar

DIRECTIONS

1. Place all ingredients, except brown sugar, into the pressure cooker; secure lid.
2. Press soup function; press start.
3. When cook time is complete, and pressure is fully vented, open lid.
4. Transfer ribs to a broiler pan, bone-side down.
5. Preheat broiler on high.
6. Press brown/sauté function to reduce liquid; let cook with the lid off until the liquid turns into a syrup-like glaze.
7. While the liquid is reducing, rub the meat side of the ribs with brown sugar and put under the broiler for 10 minutes or until golden brown.
8. Pour some glaze over the ribs and serve with additional glaze on the side.

TIP

If you don't have fresh ginger, the bottled variety commonly found in the sushi section of your supermarket is a perfect substitute.

NUTRITION FACTS

Serving Size:
1/2 of a recipe.

Amount Per Serving	% Daily Value
Calories: 210	11%
Calories from Fat: 123	18%
Total Fat: 14g	22%
Saturated Fat: 2g	10%
Cholesterol: 0mg	0%
Sodium: 747mg	31%
Total Carbohydrates: 19g	6%
Fiber: 1g	4%
Sugars: 16g	
Protein: 4g	7%
Vitamin A:	1%
Vitamin C:	10%
Calcium:	1%
Iron:	0%

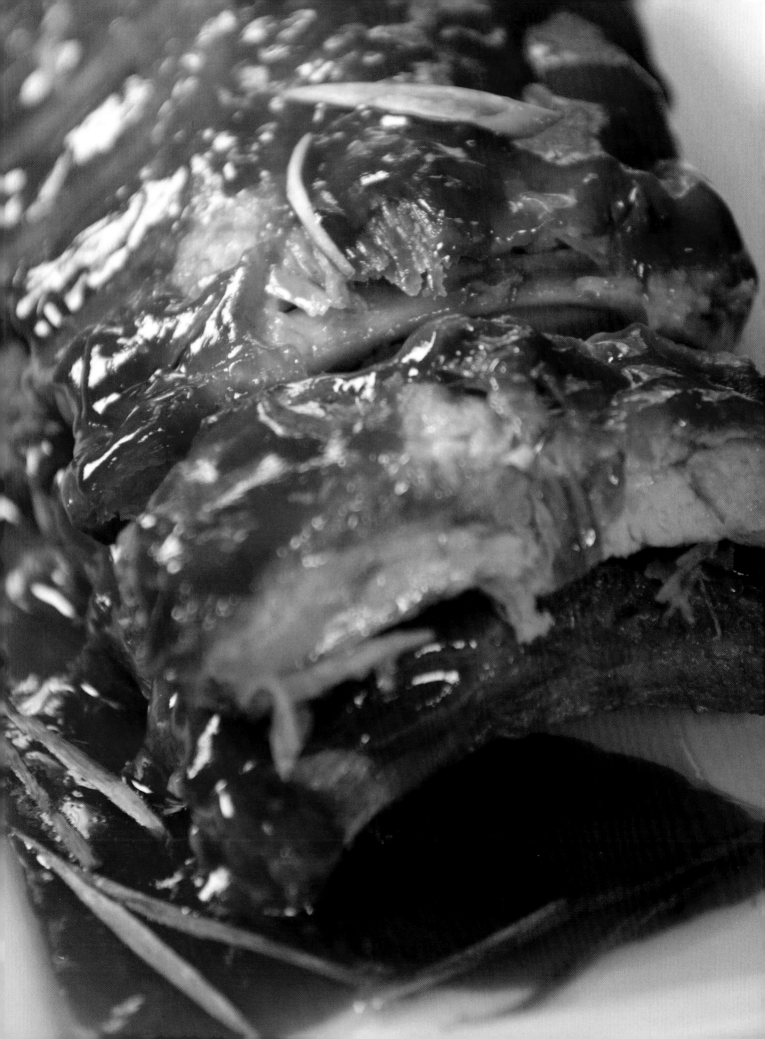

French Dip Sandwich

Servings: 4

INGREDIENTS

1 (2 pound) bottom round roast, cut into 1-inch slices

1 cup beef stock

1 tablespoon Worcestershire sauce

1 garlic clove, sliced

1 large sweet onion, quartered

1 tablespoon grape jelly

½ teaspoon salt

½ teaspoon freshly ground pepper

1 sprig thyme

4 French rolls, toasted

DIRECTIONS

1. Place all ingredients, except rolls, into the pressure cooker; secure lid.
2. Press beans function, add 15 minutes; press start.
3. When cook time is complete, and pressure is fully vented, open lid.
4. Remove thyme sprig.
5. Divide meat slices between the French rolls
6. Serve with a dish of the meat juice from the pressure cooker as a dipping sauce.

NUTRITION FACTS

Serving Size:
1/4 of a recipe.

Amount Per Serving	% Daily Value
Calories: 60	3%
Calories from Fat: 17	3%
Total Fat: 2g	3%
Saturated Fat: 1g	5%
Cholesterol: 18mg	6%
Sodium: 454mg	19%
Total Carbohydrates: 4g	1%
Fiber: 0g	0%
Sugars: 3g	
Protein: 7g	13%
Vitamin A:	0%
Vitamin C:	0%
Calcium:	0%
Iron:	4%

Holiday Brisket with Root Veggies

Servings: 4

INGREDIENTS

2 tablespoons extra-virgin olive oil

1 (3 pound) first cut brisket

1 teaspoon salt

1 teaspoon freshly ground pepper

½ cup port wine

1 cup sweet onion, sliced

1 sprig fresh thyme

½ cup celery root, peeled and diced

4 allspice berries

1 bay leaf

1 cup beef stock

1 tablespoon tomato paste

½ cup carrots, peeled and sliced

½ cup parsnips, peeled and sliced

DIRECTIONS

1. Press browning function, add oil and preheat.
2. Season the brisket with salt and pepper.
3. Add the brisket to the sauté pan and brown 3 minutes on each side.
4. Transfer brisket to platter, drain off excess oil.
5. Add wine and stock to deglaze the pan; scrape up all the little bits from the bottom of the pressure cooker.
6. Add onions, thyme, allspice berries, bay leaf, stock, and tomato paste to the pressure cooker; secure lid.
7. Press beans function, add 20 minutes; press start.
8. When cook time is complete, and pressure is fully vented, open lid.
9. Discard the thyme sprig and bay leaf.
10. Add remaining ingredients to the pressure cooker; secure lid.
11. Press vegetable function; press start.
12. When cook time is complete, and pressure is fully vented, open lid.
13. Cut the brisket against the grain and serve.

NUTRITION FACTS

Serving Size:
1/4 of a recipe.

Amount Per Serving	% Daily Value
Calories: 110	6%
Calories from Fat: 77	12%
Total Fat: 9g	14%
Saturated Fat: 2g	10%
Cholesterol: 18mg	6%
Sodium: 740mg	31%
Total Carbohydrates: 1g	0%
Fiber: 0g	0%
Sugars: 1g	
Protein: 7g	13%
Vitamin A:	1%
Vitamin C:	1%
Calcium:	0%
Iron:	4%

Pork Carnitas

Servings: 4

INGREDIENTS

2 pounds boneless pork center ribs, cut into 2-inch cubes

1 teaspoon ground cumin

½ cup chicken stock

2 garlic cloves, chopped

1 small onion, diced

1 bay leaf

1 sprig thyme

1 teaspoon salt

½ teaspoon black pepper

lettuce leaves

salsa

DIRECTIONS

1. Place all ingredients, except lettuce leaves and salsa into pressure cooker; secure lid.
2. Press beans function; press start.
3. When cooking is complete, and pressure is fully vented, open lid.
4. Remove bay leaf and thyme.

TIP

Use this tasty meat for tacos with all the trimmings.

NUTRITION FACTS

Serving Size:
1/4 of a recipe.

Amount Per Serving	% Daily Value
Calories: 5	0%
Calories from Fat: 0	0%
Total Fat: 0g	0%
Saturated Fat: 0g	0%
Cholesterol: 0mg	0%
Sodium: 593mg	25%
Total Carbohydrates: 1g	0%
Fiber: 0g	0%
Sugars: 0g	
Protein: 0g	0%
Vitamin A:	0%
Vitamin C:	5%
Calcium:	0%
Iron:	0%

Stuffed Flank Steak

Servings: 4

INGREDIENTS

2 pounds flank steak
1 bell pepper, cut into strips
1 small onion, cut into strips
3 slices mozzarella cheese
butcher's twine
1 tablespoon extra-virgin olive oil
1 teaspoon Italian seasoning
1 teaspoon salt
½ teaspoon freshly ground pepper
2 cups beef stock
1 can (14.5 ounces) Italian seasoned tomatoes

DIRECTIONS

1. Open the steak and place the peppers, onions, and cheese on the steak.
2. Roll up the steak then tie it with twine.
3. Rub the roll with oil, Italian seasoning, salt and pepper.
4. Add roll, stock and stewed tomatoes to the pressure cooker; secure lid.
5. Press beans function, add 5 minutes; press start.
6. When cook time is complete, and pressure is fully vented, open lid.
7. Remove the roll, discard the twine then cut the steak into ½-inch slices.
8. Place steak slices on a platter, top with sauce from the pressure cooker and serve.

TIP

Serve with rice or pasta.

NUTRITION FACTS

Serving Size:
1/4 of a recipe.

Amount Per Serving	% Daily Value
Calories: 188	9%
Calories from Fat: 100	15%
Total Fat: 12g	18%
Saturated Fat: 4g	20%
Cholesterol: 48mg	16%
Sodium: 1028mg	43%
Total Carbohydrates: 3g	1%
Fiber: 0g	0%
Sugars: 1g	
Protein: 19g	35%
Vitamin A:	3%
Vitamin C:	5%
Calcium:	15%
Iron:	7%

Pantry Freezer Pasta

Servings: 6

INGREDIENTS

1 pound frozen ground beef

3 cups dry penne or ziti pasta

2 ½ cups beef stock

3 cups pasta sauce

1 teaspoon salt

½ teaspoon freshly ground pepper

1 teaspoon Italian seasoning

½ teaspoon garlic powder

½ cup mozzarella cheese, shredded

DIRECTIONS

1. Place all ingredients in the pressure cooker; secure lid.
2. Press meat function, plus 5 minutes; press start.
3. When cook time is complete, and pressure is fully vented, open lid.
4. Break meat apart using a rubber spatula, stir and serve.

NUTRITION FACTS

Serving Size:
1/6 of a recipe.

Amount Per Serving	% Daily Value
Calories: 436	22%
Calories from Fat: 71	11%
Total Fat: 17g	26%
Saturated Fat: 9g	45%
Cholesterol: 77mg	26%
Sodium: 683mg	28%
Total Carbohydrates: 42g	14%
Fiber: 2g	8%
Sugars: 3g	
Protein: 31g	56%
Vitamin A:	0%
Vitamin C:	0%
Calcium:	0%
Iron:	22%

Buffalo Chicken Macaroni and Cheese

Servings: 4

INGREDIENTS

6 frozen chicken tenders

3 cups dry rigatoni pasta

3 cups chicken stock

1 small onion, chopped

2 celery stalks, chopped

1 large carrot, peeled and chopped

⅔ cup buffalo wing sauce

1 tablespoon ranch seasoning (optional)

½ cup cream cheese

1 cup sharp cheddar cheese, shredded

1 cup Swiss cheese, shredded

½ cup Gorgonzola cheese, crumbled and divided

1 cup cheddar French fried onions, crushed

DIRECTIONS

1. Place chicken, pasta, stock, onions, celery, carrots, wing sauce and ranch seasoning into the pressure cooker; secure lid.
2. Press rice function plus 5 minutes, press start.
3. When cook time is complete, and pressure is fully vented, open lid.
4. Add cream cheese to the pressure cooker; stir until dissolved.
5. Add cheddar cheese, Swiss cheese and ¼ cup Gorgonzola cheese to the pressure cooker; stir until dissolved.
6. Top with French fried onion crumbs and remaining Gorgonzola before serving.

NUTRITION FACTS

Serving Size:
1/4 of a recipe.

Amount Per Serving	% Daily Value
Calories: 618	31%
Calories from Fat: 81	12%
Total Fat: 9g	14%
Saturated Fat: 3g	15%
Cholesterol: 108mg	36%
Sodium: 1126mg	47%
Total Carbohydrates: 71g	24%
Fiber: 7g	28%
Sugars: 3g	
Protein: 69g	125%
Vitamin A:	3%
Vitamin C:	38%
Calcium:	16%
Iron:	21%

Chicken & Yellow Rice

Servings: 8

INGREDIENTS

1 bag (16 ounces) yellow rice

4 boneless skinless chicken breasts, cubed

2 tablespoons extra-virgin olive oil

1 teaspoon salt

½ teaspoon freshly ground pepper

4 cups water

1 cup frozen peas

½ cup Spanish olives

DIRECTIONS

1. Place all ingredients, except olives, into the pressure cooker; secure lid.
2. Press grains function, add 5 minutes; press start.
3. When cook time is complete, and pressure is fully vented, open lid.
4. Add the olives, stir and serve.

NUTRITION FACTS

Serving Size:
1/8 of a recipe.

Amount Per Serving	% Daily Value
Calories: 74	4%
Calories from Fat: 31	5%
Total Fat: 5g	8%
Saturated Fat: 1g	5%
Cholesterol: 0mg	0%
Sodium: 388mg	16%
Total Carbohydrates: 6g	2%
Fiber: 1g	4%
Sugars: 0g	
Protein: 2g	4%
Vitamin A:	0%
Vitamin C:	1%
Calcium:	1%
Iron:	3%

Brown Rice Pilaf with Lentils

Servings: 4

INGREDIENTS

1 cup brown basmati rice, uncooked

1 cup water

1 teaspoon salt

1 tablespoon extra-virgin olive oil

1 cup lentils

2 garlic cloves, minced

2 carrots, peeled and diced

1 medium onion, diced

1 cup tomatoes, diced

2 cups vegetable stock

1 tablespoon parsley, chopped

DIRECTIONS

1. Place rice, water salt and oil in pressure cooker; secure lid.
2. Press rice function; press start.
3. When cook time is complete, and pressure is fully released, open lid.
4. Add remaining ingredients to pressure cooker, except parsley; secure lid.
5. Press soup function; press start.
6. When cook time is complete, and pressure is fully released, open lid.
7. Stir well and top with parsley and serve.

NUTRITION FACTS

Serving Size:
1/4 of a recipe.

Amount Per Serving	% Daily Value
Calories: 250	13%
Calories from Fat: 34	5%
Total Fat: 4g	6%
Saturated Fat: 1g	5%
Cholesterol: 0mg	0%
Sodium: 609mg	25%
Total Carbohydrates: 53g	18%
Fiber: 10g	40%
Sugars: 0g	
Protein: 0g	0%
Vitamin A:	0%
Vitamin C:	5%
Calcium:	2%
Iron:	21%

Cheesy Risotto with Broccoli

Servings: 4

INGREDIENTS

2 tablespoons extra-virgin olive oil

1 small onion, chopped

1 cup Arborio rice

1 teaspoon salt

½ teaspoon white pepper

1 cup chicken stock

1 cup milk

1 cup cheddar cheese, shredded

¾ cup broccoli florets

DIRECTIONS

1. Place all ingredients except cheese and broccoli into the pressure cooker; secure lid.
2. Press fish function, add 1 minute; press start.
3. When cook time is complete, and pressure had been fully vented, open lid.
4. Add cheese and stir well.
5. Add broccoli to pressure cooker; secure lid.
6. Press fish function; press start.
7. When cook time is complete, and pressure is fully vented, open lid.
8. Serve immediately.

NUTRITION FACTS

Serving Size:
1/4 of a recipe.

Amount Per Serving	% Daily Value
Calories: 263	13%
Calories from Fat: 78	12%
Total Fat: 9g	14%
Saturated Fat: 2g	10%
Cholesterol: 5mg	2%
Sodium: 835mg	35%
Total Carbohydrates: 38g	13%
Fiber: 3g	12%
Sugars: 3g	
Protein: 5g	9%
Vitamin A:	5%
Vitamin C:	74%
Calcium:	11%
Iron:	7%

Macaroni & Cheese

Servings: 4

INGREDIENTS

2 ½ cups dry elbow macaroni

2 cups chicken stock

½ cup heavy cream

1 teaspoon salt

1 teaspoon freshly ground pepper

1 tablespoon butter

½ cup whole milk

1 ½ cups cheddar cheese, shredded

1 ½ cups mozzarella cheese, shredded

DIRECTIONS

1. Place macaroni, stock, cream, salt and pepper into the pressure cooker; secure lid.
2. Press rice function, press start.
3. When cook time is complete, and pressure is fully vented, open lid.
4. Add remaining ingredients to the pressure cooker and stir until creamy.
5. Serve immediately.

NUTRITION FACTS

Serving Size:
1/4 of a recipe.

Amount Per Serving	% Daily Value
Calories: 390	20%
Calories from Fat: 236	35%
Total Fat: 29g	45%
Saturated Fat: 12g	60%
Cholesterol: 90mg	30%
Sodium: 1004mg	42%
Total Carbohydrates: 26g	9%
Fiber: 4g	16%
Sugars: 2g	
Protein: 9g	16%
Vitamin A:	19%
Vitamin C:	1%
Calcium:	4%
Iron:	0%

Pasta with Hot Italian Sausage

Servings: 4

INGREDIENTS

1 pound hot Italian sausage, in casings

½ cup water

2 cups dry rigatoni pasta

3 cups chicken stock

3 cups pasta sauce

2 cups ricotta cheese

2 cups mozzarella cheese, shredded

1 teaspoon garlic powder

1 teaspoon salt

1 teaspoon freshly ground pepper

DIRECTIONS

1. Place sausage and water into the pressure cooker; secure lid.
2. Press rice function, minus 2 minutes; press start.
3. When cooking is complete, and pressure is fully vented, open lid.
4. Remove sausage and drain excess liquid.
5. Slice sausage, and put back in pressure cooker.
6. Add remaining ingredients to pressure cooker; secure lid.
7. Press grain function, add 5 minutes; press start.
8. When cook time is complete, and pressure is fully vented, open lid.
9. Serve immediately.

NUTRITION FACTS

Serving Size:
1/4 of a recipe.

Amount Per Serving	% Daily Value
Calories: 1432	72%
Calories from Fat: 248	37%
Total Fat: 27g	42%
Saturated Fat: 9g	45%
Cholesterol: 85mg	28%
Sodium: 2164mg	90%
Total Carbohydrates: 50g	17%
Fiber: 2g	8%
Sugars: 6g	
Protein: 24g	44%
Vitamin A:	12%
Vitamin C:	0%
Calcium:	40%
Iron:	14%

Steel Cut Oats

Servings: 4

INGREDIENTS

1 cup steel cut oats

1 ⅔ cups water

pinch of salt

1 cinnamon stick

¼ cup soy milk

2 teaspoons agave syrup

DIRECTIONS

1. Place all ingredients into the pressure cooker; secure lid.
2. Press vegetable function, add 1 minute; press start.
3. When cook time is complete, and pressure is fully vented, open lid.
4. Remove the cinnamon stick and serve.

NUTRITION FACTS

Serving Size:
1/4 of a recipe.

Amount Per Serving	% Daily Value
Calories: 79	4%
Calories from Fat: 13	2%
Total Fat: 2g	3%
Saturated Fat: 0g	0%
Cholesterol: 0mg	0%
Sodium: 42mg	2%
Total Carbohydrates: 14g	5%
Fiber: 2g	8%
Sugars: 1g	
Protein: 3g	5%
Vitamin A:	1%
Vitamin C:	0%
Calcium:	1%
Iron:	5%

Perfect Brown Rice

Servings: 7

INGREDIENTS

1 pound long grained brown rice, uncooked

5 cups water

1 teaspoon salt

1 tablespoon extra-virgin olive oil

DIRECTIONS

1. Rinse rice, place into pressure cooker.
2. Add remaining ingredients to pressure cooker; secure lid.
3. Press grain function, add 5 minutes; press start.
4. When cook time is complete, and pressure is fully vented, open lid.
5. Serve immediately.

NUTRITION FACTS

Serving Size:
1/7 of a recipe.

Amount Per Serving	% Daily Value
Calories: 236	12%
Calories from Fat: 40	6%
Total Fat: 5g	8%
Saturated Fat: 0g	0%
Cholesterol: 0mg	0%
Sodium: 337mg	14%
Total Carbohydrates: 48g	16%
Fiber: 4g	16%
Sugars: 0g	
Protein: 4g	7%
Vitamin A:	0%
Vitamin C:	0%
Calcium:	0%
Iron:	0%

Red Beans with Rice

Servings: 4

INGREDIENTS

4 cups cooked rice
1 pound dried red kidney beans, rinsed
1 large onion, diced
1 large bell pepper, diced
4 garlic cloves, minced
1 large, smoked ham hock
1 ½ pounds mild smoked sausage, sliced
2 teaspoons thyme
2 bay leaves
2 tablespoons parsley, chopped
½ teaspoon salt
½ teaspoon fresh ground pepper
½ teaspoon cayenne pepper
1 tablespoon hot sauce
1 teaspoon Worcestershire sauce
8 cups chicken stock

DIRECTIONS

1. Place all ingredients, except rice, into pressure cooker; secure lid.
2. Press soup function, add 5 minutes; press start.
3. When cook time is complete, and pressure is fully vented, open lid
4. Serve over rice.

NUTRITION FACTS

Serving Size:
1/4 of a recipe.

Amount Per Serving	% Daily Value
Calories: 1089	54%
Calories from Fat: 320	48%
Total Fat: 35g	54%
Saturated Fat: 0g	0%
Cholesterol: 70mg	23%
Sodium: 3121mg	130%
Total Carbohydrates: 159g	53%
Fiber: 9g	36%
Sugars: 9g	
Protein: 30g	55%
Vitamin A:	0%
Vitamin C:	13%
Calcium:	14%
Iron:	38%

Reisfleisch

Servings: 6

INGREDIENTS

1 tablespoon extra-virgin olive oil

1 medium onion, diced

1 red bell pepper, diced

3 garlic cloves, minced

2 tablespoons tomato paste

1 teaspoon salt

½ teaspoon cayenne pepper

1 teaspoon ground cumin

1 tablespoon Hungarian paprika

½ teaspoon black pepper

1 pound smoked sausage, thinly sliced

½ teaspoon marjoram

2 cups long-grain rice, rinsed

4 cups beef stock

DIRECTIONS

1. Press browning function; pour oil into pressure cooker and let it preheat with the lid off.
2. Add onions to the pressure cooker and cook for 2 minutes, stirring occasionally.
3. Add the red peppers and garlic to the pressure cooker; stir.
4. Add tomato paste to the pressure cooker and cook for an additional 2 minutes.
5. Add remaining ingredients to the pressure cooker; secure lid.
6. Press vegetable function, add 1 minute; press start.
7. When cook time is complete, and pressure is fully vented, open lid.
8. Stir and serve immediately.

NUTRITION FACTS

Serving Size:
1/6 of a recipe.

Amount Per Serving	% Daily Value
Calories: 665	33%
Calories from Fat: 323	48%
Total Fat: 36g	55%
Saturated Fat: 13g	65%
Cholesterol: 122mg	41%
Sodium: 1530mg	64%
Total Carbohydrates: 46g	15%
Fiber: 1g	4%
Sugars: 2g	
Protein: 30g	55%
Vitamin A:	21%
Vitamin C:	5%
Calcium:	2%
Iron:	26%

Wild Rice with Mushrooms

Servings: 4

INGREDIENTS

2 cups wild rice, uncooked

4 cups beef broth

1 cup mushrooms

1 small onion, diced

2 tablespoons butter

½ cup almonds, slivered

2 tablespoons green onions, chopped

DIRECTIONS

1. Place rice, stock, mushrooms and onions into pressure cooker; secure lid.
2. Press meat function, add 5 minutes; Press start.
3. When cooking is complete, and pressure is fully vented, open lid.
4. Add almonds and butter; stir.
5. Garnish with green onions and serve.

NUTRITION FACTS

Serving Size:
1/4 of a recipe.

Amount Per Serving	% Daily Value
Calories: 404	20%
Calories from Fat: 70	11%
Total Fat: 6g	9%
Saturated Fat: 3g	15%
Cholesterol: 15mg	5%
Sodium: 1848mg	77%
Total Carbohydrates: 75g	25%
Fiber: 6g	24%
Sugars: 0g	
Protein: 17g	31%
Vitamin A:	4%
Vitamin C:	7%
Calcium:	0%
Iron:	8%

Asian Chicken Curry

Servings: 4

INGREDIENTS

2 pounds skinless chicken legs

1 cup chicken stock

¼ cup brown sugar

1 tablespoon curry powder

1 teaspoon garam masala

1 medium onion, chopped

1 red bell pepper, julienned

1 can (14.5 ounces) petite diced tomatoes

1 cup plain yogurt

1 tablespoon fresh cilantro leaves, chopped

DIRECTIONS

1. Place all ingredients, except yogurt and cilantro, into pressure cooker.
2. Press soup function; press start.
3. When cook time is complete, and pressure is fully vented, open lid.
4. Transfer chicken to a platter.
5. Add yogurt to the stock inside the pressure cooker; stir.
6. Pour mixture over chicken, top with cilantro and serve.

NUTRITION FACTS

Serving Size:
1/4 of a recipe.

Amount Per Serving	% Daily Value
Calories: 229	11%
Calories from Fat: 23	3%
Total Fat: 2g	3%
Saturated Fat: 0g	0%
Cholesterol: 51mg	17%
Sodium: 558mg	23%
Total Carbohydrates: 18g	6%
Fiber: 0g	0%
Sugars: 16g	
Protein: 35g	64%
Vitamin A:	0%
Vitamin C:	6%
Calcium:	9%
Iron:	0%

Chicken Enchilada Casserole

Servings: 4

INGREDIENTS

2 pounds boneless skinless chicken breasts

1 can (4 ounces) green chiles, chopped

1 envelope taco seasoning

1 cup chicken stock

1 can (10 ounce) enchilada sauce

1 cup Colby and cheddar cheese blend, shredded

3 green onions, chopped

Sour cream

DIRECTIONS

1. Place chicken, chilies, taco seasoning, stock, and tortilla soup into the pressure cooker; secure lid.
2. Press grain function; press start.
3. When cook time is complete, and pressure is fully vented, open lid.
4. Add the tortilla chips, enchilada sauce and cheese; stir and secure lid.
5. Press fish function, minus 2 minutes; press start.
6. When cook time is complete, and pressure is fully vented, open lid.
7. Garnish with green onions and sour cream.
8. Serve immediately.

NUTRITION FACTS

Serving Size:
1/4 of a recipe.

Amount Per Serving	% Daily Value
Calories: 144	7%
Calories from Fat: 26	4%
Total Fat: 3g	5%
Saturated Fat: 1g	5%
Cholesterol: 47mg	16%
Sodium: 398mg	17%
Total Carbohydrates: 6g	2%
Fiber: 0g	0%
Sugars: 0g	
Protein: 18g	33%
Vitamin A:	18%
Vitamin C:	120%
Calcium:	0%
Iron:	34%

Chipotle Chicken Burrito

Servings: 4

INGREDIENTS

4 boneless skinless chicken breasts, chopped into 1-inch pieces

1 cup chicken stock

2 wholes chipotles in adobo sauce

1 teaspoon cumin seeds

1 teaspoon salt

1 teaspoon cayenne pepper

1 teaspoon sugar

1 can (10 ounces) Mexican tomatoes with green chilies and lime

1 cup jasmine rice

1 cup black beans, cooked

½ cup cheddar cheese, shredded

2 tablespoons fresh cilantro, chopped

6 (12-inches each) flour tortillas

DIRECTIONS

1. Place all ingredients, except tortillas, into the pressure cooker; secure lid.
2. Press rice function, minus 2 minutes; press start.
3. When cook time is complete, and pressure is fully vented, open lid.
4. Assemble the burritos by spooning the chicken mixture down the center of each tortilla and rolling them into burritos.

TIP

To make them even more delicious, serve the burritos with lettuce, avocado and sour cream.

NUTRITION FACTS

Serving Size:
1/4 of a recipe.

Amount Per Serving	% Daily Value
Calories: 405	20%
Calories from Fat: 50	8%
Total Fat: 6g	9%
Saturated Fat: 1g	5%
Cholesterol: 0mg	0%
Sodium: 1505mg	63%
Total Carbohydrates: 77g	26%
Fiber: 3g	12%
Sugars: 1g	
Protein: 10g	18%
Vitamin A:	0%
Vitamin C:	0%
Calcium:	13%
Iron:	17%

Coq au Vin

Servings: 6

INGREDIENTS

1 whole chicken, cut into pieces

1 tablespoon flour

1 teaspoon salt

½ teaspoon freshly ground pepper

2 bacon strips diced

2 tablespoons butter

8 boiler onions, peeled

1 pound whole mushrooms

2 sprigs of thyme

2 cups dry red wine

1 cup chicken stock

1 teaspoon sugar

DIRECTIONS

1. Rub the chicken with flour, salt and pepper.
2. Press brown/sauté function and preheat pressure cooker; add bacon and cook until crisp.
3. Add butter to the pressure cooker and let it melt.
4. Add chicken pieces to the skillet and cook until golden brown.
5. Add remaining ingredients to pressure cooker; secure lid.
6. Press beans function; press start.
7. When cook time is complete, and pressure is fully vented, open lid.
8. Transfer chicken, onions and mushrooms to a platter.
9. With lid off, press brown/sauté function and let liquid reduce for 10 minutes.
10. Ladle sauce over the chicken and serve.

NUTRITION FACTS

Serving Size:
1/6 of a recipe.

Amount Per Serving	% Daily Value
Calories: 97	5%
Calories from Fat: 35	5%
Total Fat: 4g	6%
Saturated Fat: 0g	0%
Cholesterol: 10mg	3%
Sodium: 558mg	23%
Total Carbohydrates: 11g	4%
Fiber: 2g	8%
Sugars: 1g	
Protein: 5g	9%
Vitamin A:	3%
Vitamin C:	28%
Calcium:	0%
Iron:	0%

Chicken with Sweet Potato Dumplings

Servings: 6

INGREDIENTS

6 chicken thighs bone-in, without skin
1 teaspoon kosher salt
1 teaspoon freshly ground pepper
½ teaspoon rosemary leaves, chopped
1 tablespoon extra-virgin olive oil
¼ cup white wine
1 cup chicken stock
½ cup pearl onion
1 celery stalk, sliced
1 large carrot, peeled and sliced
¼ cup tiny frozen peas
1 sprig fresh thyme
½ teaspoon salt
½ teaspoon dried sage
1 ¼ cups unbleached flour
1 cup mashed, sweet potato
1 ½ cups buttermilk

DIRECTIONS

1. Season both sides of the chicken with kosher salt, pepper and rosemary.
2. Press brown/sauté function, add oil and preheat pressure cooker.
3. Place chicken into the pan; brown for 3 minutes on each side.
4. Remove chicken to a platter; cover.
5. Add wine and stock to the pressure cooker to deglaze; scrape up all the little bits from the bottom of the pan.
6. Add chicken, wine, stock, onions, celery, carrot, thyme and peas to the pressure cooker; secure lid.
7. Press soup function; press start.
8. While cooking, combine flour, sweet potatoes, buttermilk, salt, baking powder and sage in a bowl; mix well.
9. When cook time is complete, and pressure is fully vented, open lid.
10. Discard thyme sprig.
11. With the lid off, press brown/sauté function.
12. While simmering, drop dumplings by the spoonful into the pressure cooker.
13. Cook dumplings for 3 minutes on each side before serving.

NUTRITION FACTS

Serving Size:
1/6 of a recipe.

Amount Per Serving	% Daily Value
Calories: 267	13%
Calories from Fat: 96	14%
Total Fat: 11g	17%
Saturated Fat: 3g	15%
Cholesterol: 46mg	15%
Sodium: 884mg	37%
Total Carbohydrates: 25g	8%
Fiber: 0g	0%
Sugars: 3g	
Protein: 6g	11%
Vitamin A:	2%
Vitamin C:	0%
Calcium:	9%
Iron:	10%

Tangy Tender Barbeque Chicken

Servings: 4

INGREDIENTS

1 whole chicken, cut into 8 pieces

½ cup chicken stock

1 teaspoon salt

1 teaspoon freshly ground pepper

1 teaspoon dry mustard

1 teaspoon paprika

1 medium onion, diced

3 garlic cloves, minced

2 tablespoons cider vinegar

¼ cup maple syrup

¼ cup ketchup

¼ cup molasses

DIRECTIONS

1. Place all ingredients into the pressure cooker; secure lid.
2. Press grain function, add 5 minutes; press start
3. When cook time is complete, and pressure is fully vented, open lid.
4. Transfer the chicken to a broiler pan, bone side down.
5. Preheat the broiler on high.
6. To reduce the cooking liquid in the pressure cooker, press brown/sauté function; let cook with lid off until the liquid turns into a syrup like glaze.
7. While liquid is reducing, place the chicken under the broiler for 7 minutes on each side.
8. Pour barbecue sauce over the chicken and serve with additional sauce on the side.

NUTRITION FACTS

Serving Size:
1/4 of a recipe.

Amount Per Serving	% Daily Value
Calories: 137	7%
Calories from Fat: 1	0%
Total Fat: 0g	0%
Saturated Fat: 0g	0%
Cholesterol: 0mg	0%
Sodium: 938mg	39%
Total Carbohydrates: 32g	11%
Fiber: 0g	0%
Sugars: 14g	
Protein: 2g	4%
Vitamin A:	10%
Vitamin C:	5%
Calcium:	0%
Iron:	0%

Moroccan Chicken

Servings: 4

INGREDIENTS

3 pounds skinless bone-in chicken pieces

2 tablespoons extra-virgin olive oil

1 teaspoon salt

1 teaspoon cumin seeds

1 teaspoon nigella seeds (optional)

1 cup chicken stock

1 medium onion, sliced

3 saffron strands

1 teaspoon turmeric powder

1 tablespoon lemon zest

¼ cup lemon juice

12 black olives, pitted

2 tablespoons fresh cilantro, chopped

DIRECTIONS

1. Pat chicken dry using paper towels.
2. Press brown/sauté function, add oil and preheat pressure cooker.
3. Place chicken pieces into the pressure cooker; season with salt, cumin and nigella seeds.
4. Cook the chicken for 3 minutes on each side or until browned.
5. Remove chicken to a platter and cover.
6. Add stock to the pressure cooker; scrape up little bits from the bottom.
7. Add remaining ingredients, except cilantro, to the pressure cooker; secure lid.
8. Press grains function, add five minutes; press start.
9. When cook time is complete, and pressure is fully vented, open lid.
10. Top chicken with cilantro and serve.

NUTRITION FACTS

Serving Size:
1/4 of a recipe.

Amount Per Serving	% Daily Value
Calories: 288	14%
Calories from Fat: 93	14%
Total Fat: 11g	17%
Saturated Fat: 1g	5%
Cholesterol: 75mg	25%
Sodium: 1183mg	49%
Total Carbohydrates: 2g	1%
Fiber: 0g	0%
Sugars: 0g	
Protein: 46g	84%
Vitamin A:	0%
Vitamin C:	5%
Calcium:	0%
Iron:	0%

Easy Chicken Marsala

Servings: 4

INGREDIENTS

4 frozen boneless skinless chicken breasts

1 cup mushrooms, sliced

1 shallot, sliced

½ cup chicken stock

½ cup marsala wine

1 sprig thyme

1 teaspoon salt

½ teaspoon freshly ground pepper

1 envelope brown gravy mix

DIRECTIONS

1. Place all ingredients into the pressure cooker; secure lid.
2. Press grain function, add 5 minutes; press start.
3. Remove thyme sprig.
4. Transfer chicken to a platter, pour sauce over chicken and serve.

NUTRITION FACTS

Serving Size:
1/4 of a recipe.

Amount Per Serving	% Daily Value
Calories: 23	1%
Calories from Fat: 1	0%
Total Fat: 0g	0%
Saturated Fat: 0g	0%
Cholesterol: 0mg	0%
Sodium: 679mg	28%
Total Carbohydrates: 2g	1%
Fiber: 0g	0%
Sugars: 0g	
Protein: 3g	5%
Vitamin A:	0%
Vitamin C:	2%
Calcium:	0%
Iron:	0%

Quinoa Turkey Meatloaf

Servings: 4

INGREDIENTS

- ⅓ cup quinoa, cooked
- ⅔ cup chicken stock
- 1 medium onion, chopped
- 1 sprig tarragon
- 4 ounces mushrooms, sliced
- 1 tablespoon Worcestershire sauce
- 1 pound ground turkey
- 1 teaspoon salt
- ¼ teaspoon granulated garlic
- ½ teaspoon freshly ground pepper
- 1 large egg, beaten
- 1 cup tomato sauce
- ¼ cup brown sugar

DIRECTIONS

1. In a bowl, combine all ingredients, except tomato sauce and brown sugar; mix well using your hands.
2. Place meatloaf mixture into the pressure cooker.
3. In a bowl, combine the tomato sauce and brown sugar the pour it over the meatloaf; secure lid.
4. Press meat function, add 5 minutes; press start.
5. When cook time is complete, and pressure is fully vented, open lid.
6. Serve immediately.

NUTRITION FACTS

Serving Size:
1/4 of a recipe.

Amount Per Serving	% Daily Value
Calories: 243	12%
Calories from Fat: 8	1%
Total Fat: 2g	3%
Saturated Fat: 0g	0%
Cholesterol: 106mg	35%
Sodium: 1164mg	49%
Total Carbohydrates: 18g	6%
Fiber: 1g	4%
Sugars: 15g	
Protein: 20g	36%
Vitamin A:	7%
Vitamin C:	16%
Calcium:	0%
Iron:	1%

Turkey Pot Roast

Servings: 4

INGREDIENTS

1 (4 pound) boneless turkey beast, rinsed

½ cup amber beer

½ teaspoon sea salt

½ cup chicken stock

½ teaspoon freshly ground pepper

1 tablespoon tomato paste

½ teaspoon poultry seasoning

2 celery stalks, diced

1 tablespoon extra-virgin olive oil

2 sprigs fresh thyme

1 medium onion, quartered

4 bliss potatoes, halved

¼ cup mushrooms, sliced

3 carrots, peeled, cut into 2-inch pieces

DIRECTIONS

1. Pat the turkey breast dry using paper towels.
2. Rub turkey breast with salt, pepper and poultry seasoning.
3. Press brown/sauté function, add oil to pressure cooker and preheat.
4. Gently place turkey breast into the skillet; sear until all sides are golden brown.
5. Transfer turkey breast to a platter and cover.
6. Place onions and mushrooms into the skillet; cook for 2 minutes.
7. Add beer and stock to deglaze the skillet; scrape up all the little bits from the bottom of the pressure cooker.
8. Add tomato paste, celery and thyme to the pressure cooker; stir, then secure lid.
9. Press beans function, add 5 minutes; press start.
10. When cook time is complete, and pressure is fully vented, open lid.
11. Carefully remove the lid and add remaining ingredients to the pressure cooker; secure lid.
12. Press rice function, minus 2 minutes; press start.
13. When cook time is complete, and pressure is fully vented, open lid.
14. Remove thyme sprig and serve.

NUTRITION FACTS

Serving Size:
1/4 of a recipe.

Amount Per Serving	% Daily Value
Calories: 133	7%
Calories from Fat: 56	8%
Total Fat: 6g	9%
Saturated Fat: 1g	5%
Cholesterol: 15mg	5%
Sodium: 1047mg	44%
Total Carbohydrates: 11g	4%
Fiber: 5g	20%
Sugars: 1g	
Protein: 8g	15%
Vitamin A:	1%
Vitamin C:	37%
Calcium:	8%
Iron:	1%

Stuffed Turkey Breast

Servings: 4

INGREDIENTS

2 pounds turkey breast tenderloins, butterflied

½ teaspoon salt

¼ teaspoon poultry seasoning

1 box (6 ounces) turkey flavored stuffing mix

½ cup dried cherries

toothpicks

1 cup chicken stock

1 envelope of turkey gravy mix

DIRECTIONS

1. Sprinkle turkey with salt and poultry seasoning.
2. Prepare stuffing mix according to package directions; then add dried cherries to the stuffing.
3. Divide the stuffing between the tenderloins and place the mixture in the center of each.
4. Roll tenderloins to cover the stuffing then secure with toothpicks.
5. Add the stock and gravy envelope contents to the pressure cooker.
6. Place turkey, toothpick side down, into the pressure cooker; secure lid.
7. Press grains function, add 5 minutes; press start.
8. When cook time is complete, and pressure is fully released, open lid.
9. Transfer turkey to a cutting board.
10. Remove toothpicks, slice turkey into 1-inch rounds and serve with gravy.

TIP

Try dried cranberries instead of cherries.

NUTRITION FACTS

Serving Size:
1/4 of a recipe.

Amount Per Serving	% Daily Value
Calories: 9	0%
Calories from Fat: 3	0%
Total Fat: 0g	0%
Saturated Fat: 0g	0%
Cholesterol: 0mg	0%
Sodium: 473mg	20%
Total Carbohydrates: 0g	0%
Fiber: 0g	0%
Sugars: 0g	
Protein: 1g	2%
Vitamin A:	0%
Vitamin C:	0%
Calcium:	0%
Iron:	0%

Stuffed Turkey Peppers with Couscous

Servings: 4

INGREDIENTS

1 pound ground turkey

1 can (14.5 ounces) petite diced tomatoes

1 teaspoon salt

½ cup Israeli couscous

1 teaspoon freshly ground pepper

1 cup chicken stock

1 medium sweet onion, chopped

¼ cup Parmesan cheese, grated

3 garlic cloves, minced

4 large bell peppers, membrane removed

4 saffron threads

1 cup tomato sauce

DIRECTIONS

1. Press brown/sauté function and place the turkey in the pressure cooker.
2. With the lid off, cook turkey for 3 minutes, breaking it up using a wooden spoon.
3. Season the turkey with salt and pepper then add the onions to the pressures cooker and cook for an additional 3 minutes.
4. Add the garlic and saffron to the pressure cooker and cook for an additional minute.
5. Add tomatoes, couscous, and stock to the pressure cooker; stir then secure the lid.
6. Press vegetable function, add 1 minute; press start.
7. When cook time is complete, and pressure is fully vented, open lid.
8. Divide the turkey mixture between the peppers.
9. Rinse the pressure cooker insert, place the peppers in the pressure cooker and cover them with tomato sauce; secure lid.
10. Press vegetable function, add 1 minute; press start.
11. When cook time is complete, and pressure is fully vented, open lid.
12. Serve immediately.

NUTRITION FACTS

Serving Size:
1/4 of a recipe.

Amount Per Serving	% Daily Value
Calories: 204	10%
Calories from Fat: 25	4%
Total Fat: 4g	6%
Saturated Fat: 2g	10%
Cholesterol: 78mg	26%
Sodium: 1306mg	54%
Total Carbohydrates: 3g	1%
Fiber: 1g	4%
Sugars: 3g	
Protein: 21g	38%
Vitamin A:	6%
Vitamin C:	10%
Calcium:	9%
Iron:	0%

Thai Chicken Curry

Servings: 4

INGREDIENTS

2 cups chicken stock

1 medium onion, diced

3 garlic cloves, sliced

1 tablespoon fresh ginger, sliced

2 tablespoons Thai red curry paste

1 tablespoon lime zest

2 tablespoons fish sauce

2 pounds boneless chicken tenders

2 tablespoons brown sugar

1 red bell pepper, julienned

1 can (13.5 ounces) light coconut milk

1 can (8 ounces) bamboo shoots

2 tablespoons fresh cilantro leaves, chopped

green onions, chopped

DIRECTIONS

1. Place all ingredients, except green onions, into pressure cooker; secure lid.
2. Press rice function, minus 2 minutes; press start.
3. When cook time is complete, and pressure is fully vented, open lid.
4. Top with green onions and serve.

NUTRITION FACTS

Serving Size:
1/4 of a recipe.

Amount Per Serving	% Daily Value
Calories: 202	10%
Calories from Fat: 25	4%
Total Fat: 3g	5%
Saturated Fat: 0g	0%
Cholesterol: 50mg	17%
Sodium: 625mg	26%
Total Carbohydrates: 10g	3%
Fiber: 0g	0%
Sugars: 6g	
Protein: 33g	60%
Vitamin A:	6%
Vitamin C:	45%
Calcium:	0%
Iron:	10%

VEGETABLES AND SIDES

Buttery Corn on the Cob

Servings: 4

INGREDIENTS

6 ears of corn, husked

½ cup of water

1 teaspoon salt

½ teaspoon sugar

3 tablespoons butter

DIRECTIONS

1. Place all ingredients into pressure cooker; secure lid.
2. Press fish function, add 1 minute; press start.
3. When cook time is complete, and pressure is fully vented, open lid.
4. Stir and serve.

TIP

Add more salt and butter if desired.

NUTRITION FACTS

Serving Size:
1/4 of a recipe.

Amount Per Serving	% Daily Value
Calories: 77	4%
Calories from Fat: 75	11%
Total Fat: 8g	12%
Saturated Fat: 0g	0%
Cholesterol: 23mg	8%
Sodium: 658mg	27%
Total Carbohydrates: 1g	0%
Fiber: 0g	0%
Sugars: 1g	
Protein: 0g	0%
Vitamin A:	6%
Vitamin C:	0%
Calcium:	0%
Iron:	0%

Artichokes in Lemon Dill

Servings: 4

INGREDIENTS

3 wholes artichokes
1 cup white wine
½ cup chicken stock
Juice and zest from 1 lemon
2 sprigs fresh dill
2 garlic cloves

DIRECTIONS

1. Place artichokes, stem side up, into the pressure cooker.
2. Add remaining ingredients to the pressure cooker; secure lid.
3. Press grains function; press start.
4. When cook time is complete, and pressure is fully vented, open lid.
5. Serve hot with some broth on the side.

TIP

Chill and serve; top with your favorite vinaigrette.

NUTRITION FACTS

Serving Size:
1/4 of a recipe.

Amount Per Serving	% Daily Value
Calories: 34	2%
Calories from Fat: 1	0%
Total Fat: 0g	0%
Saturated Fat: 0g	0%
Cholesterol: 0mg	0%
Sodium: 469mg	20%
Total Carbohydrates: 6g	2%
Fiber: 0g	0%
Sugars: 0g	
Protein: 1g	2%
Vitamin A:	0%
Vitamin C:	0%
Calcium:	0%
Iron:	0%

Braised Purple Cabbage

Servings: 4

INGREDIENTS

1 head of purple cabbage, sliced

3 apples, cored and quartered

1 large onion, sliced

2 cups of chicken stock

1 teaspoon sugar

1 teaspoon salt

½ teaspoon freshly ground pepper

1 tablespoon balsamic vinegar

1 teaspoon caraway seeds

DIRECTIONS

1. Place all ingredients, except caraway seeds, into the pressure cooker; secure lid.
2. Press grains function, add 5 minutes; press start.
3. When cook time is complete, and pressure is fully vented, open lid.
4. Add caraway seeds and serve.

NUTRITION FACTS

Serving Size:
1/4 of a recipe.

Amount Per Serving	% Daily Value
Calories: 63	3%
Calories from Fat: 5	1%
Total Fat: 1g	2%
Saturated Fat: 0g	0%
Cholesterol: 0mg	0%
Sodium: 1009mg	42%
Total Carbohydrates: 9g	3%
Fiber: 4g	16%
Sugars: 1g	
Protein: 5g	9%
Vitamin A:	4%
Vitamin C:	145%
Calcium:	8%
Iron:	4%

Brussels Sprouts with Pearl Onion

Servings: 6

INGREDIENTS

1 ½ pounds Brussel sprouts, trimmed

1 bag (10 ounces) frozen pearl onions

1 cup chicken stock

1 teaspoon freshly ground pepper

1 sprig fresh thyme

DIRECTIONS

1. Place all ingredients into the pressure cooker; secure lid.
2. Press fish function, add 3 minutes; press start.
3. When cook time is complete, and pressure is fully vented, open lid.
4. Remove thyme sprig and serve.

TIP

Serve this dish with a side of horseradish sauce.

NUTRITION FACTS

Serving Size:
1/6 of a recipe.

Amount Per Serving	% Daily Value
Calories: 298	15%
Calories from Fat: 10	2%
Total Fat: 1g	2%
Saturated Fat: 0g	0%
Cholesterol: 0mg	0%
Sodium: 900mg	38%
Total Carbohydrates: 38g	13%
Fiber: 23g	90%
Sugars: 23g	
Protein: 27g	49%
Vitamin A:	45%
Vitamin C:	600%
Calcium:	15%
Iron:	15%

Josephine Cook's Stuffed Artichokes

Servings 4

INGREDIENTS

2 large artichokes, trimmed (see directions)

1 cup seasoned Italian bread crumbs

¾ cup grated Romano or Parmesan cheese

2 tbsp. extra virgin olive oil (may need more)

¼ cup chopped fresh parsley

2 cloves garlic, chopped

¼ teaspoon salt

¼ teaspoon freshly ground black pepper

1 cup water or vegetable broth

DIRECTIONS

1. Cut the bottom stem of the artichoke off. Remove the outer leaves.
2. Cut an inch off the top of the artichoke. You will see the purple leaves in the center, which can be thorny; with scissors cut the thorns off.
3. Remove the choke, but you can scoop it out, if you desire. On each leaf, there is a thorn, cut those off with a scissors.
4. Turn the artichoke upside down and press down to open the leaves for stuffing. Rinse and shake moisture out.
5. Place the artichoke on a platter and set aside.
6. In a bowl mix the Italian bread crumbs, Romano or Parmesan cheese, chopped parsley, chopped garlic, salt and pepper and 1 ½ Tbsp. extra virgin olive oil. You want a stuffing that is moist.
7. Starting with the bottom outer leaves, open them and add the stuffing. Continue around the artichoke placing the stuffing in each leaf.
8. If you have removed the center (the choke) you can fill the center with any leftover stuffing.
9. Place the artichokes on the rack, add 1 cup water or vegetable broth to the pot and drizzle the tops with some extra virgin olive oil.
10. Press soup function; press start.
11. Cooking time varies depending on the size of your artichokes.
12. When cook time is complete, and pressure is fully released, open lid.

TIP

Artichoke leaves will pull off easily when they are cooked.

NUTRITION FACTS

Serving Size:
1/4 of a recipe.

Amount Per Serving	% Daily Value
Calories: 368	18%
Calories from Fat: 270	41%
Total Fat: 27g	42%
Saturated Fat: 18g	90%
Cholesterol: 90mg	30%
Sodium: 1942mg	81%
Total Carbohydrates: 2g	1%
Fiber: 0g	1%
Sugars: 0g	
Protein: 40g	73%
Vitamin A:	0%
Vitamin C:	0%
Calcium:	108%
Iron:	2%

Josephine Cook's Kale and Chickpeas

Servings: 6

INGREDIENTS

1 pound fresh kale, washed and drained

1 stick Italian pepperoni, or Italian sausage or chopped ham

2 cups of chicken or vegetable broth

3 cloves chopped garlic

1 medium onion, sliced

2–15 ounce cans of chickpeas or white kidney beans, drained and rinsed

2 teaspoons extra virgin olive oil

¼ teaspoon salt

¼ teaspoon freshly ground black pepper

Pinch of hot pepper seeds, more if you want it spicier (Italian pepperoni can be spicy)

DIRECTIONS

1. Wash the kale and drain. Place in a bowl and add the drained chickpeas and mix.
2. Cut the pepperoni or sausage or ham into bite size pieces.
3. With the lid off the pressure cooker, add the extra virgin olive oil, pepperoni, sausage or ham, onions and garlic.
4. Press the brown/sauté function and sauté for 3 minutes, stirring.
5. Add the kale and chickpea mixture.
6. Add salt, freshly ground pepper, and hot pepper seeds, if using.
7. Add the chicken or vegetable broth; secure lid.
8. Press fish function, add 1 minute; press start.
9. When cook time is complete, and pressure is fully vented, open lid.
10. Serve immediately.

NUTRITION FACTS

Serving Size:
1/6 of a recipe.

Amount Per Serving	% Daily Value
Calories: 315	16%
Calories from Fat: 82	12%
Total Fat: 10g	15%
Saturated Fat: 1g	7%
Cholesterol: 66mg	22%
Sodium: 866mg	36%
Total Carbohydrates: 19g	6%
Fiber: 5g	19%
Sugars: 3g	
Protein: 30g	55%
Vitamin A:	0%
Vitamin C:	24%
Calcium:	4%
Iron:	7%

Mashed Potatoes with Rutabaga

Servings: 4

INGREDIENTS

6 Yukon gold potatoes, peeled and halved

½ cup rutabaga, peeled and diced into 1-inch cubes

1 cup chicken stock

1 teaspoon salt

½ teaspoon freshly ground pepper

2 tablespoons heavy cream

2 tablespoons butter

DIRECTIONS

1. Place all ingredients, except cream and butter, into the pressure cooker; secure lid.
2. Press rice function, minus 2 minutes; press start.
3. When cook time is complete, and pressure is fully vented, open lid.
4. Drain the potatoes.
5. Add cream and butter to the potatoes and mash using a potato masher.
6. Serve immediately.

NUTRITION FACTS

Serving Size:
1/4 of a recipe.

Amount Per Serving	% Daily Value
Calories: 84	4%
Calories from Fat: 78	12%
Total Fat: 9g	14%
Saturated Fat: 2g	10%
Cholesterol: 25mg	8%
Sodium: 816mg	34%
Total Carbohydrates: 0g	0%
Fiber: 0g	0%
Sugars: 0g	
Protein: 1g	2%
Vitamin A:	6%
Vitamin C:	0%
Calcium:	0%
Iron:	0%

Parsnip Puree with Shallots

Servings: 4

INGREDIENTS

2 pounds parsnips, peeled and cut into 2-inch pieces

1 shallot, minced

1/3 cup chicken stock

½ teaspoon salt

½ teaspoon freshly ground pepper

2 ounces cream cheese

DIRECTIONS

1. Place all ingredients, except cream cheese, into the pressure cooker; secure lid.
2. Press fish function, add 2 minutes; press start.
3. When cook time is complete, and pressure is fully vented, open lid.
4. Strain the parsnips; then place them into a food processor.
5. Add cream cheese to the food processor and puree until smooth.
6. Serve immediately.

NUTRITION FACTS

Serving Size:
1/4 of a recipe.

Amount Per Serving	% Daily Value
Calories: 186	9%
Calories from Fat: 46	7%
Total Fat: 5g	8%
Saturated Fat: 3g	15%
Cholesterol: 15mg	5%
Sodium: 418mg	17%
Total Carbohydrates: 34g	11%
Fiber: 9g	36%
Sugars: 0g	
Protein: 4g	7%
Vitamin A:	3%
Vitamin C:	0%
Calcium:	0%
Iron:	0%

Spaghetti Squash

Servings: 4

INGREDIENTS

1 large spaghetti squash, seeds removed and cut horizontally

2 tablespoons butter, divided

¼ teaspoon kosher, salt

¼ teaspoon white pepper

2 cups water

DIRECTIONS

1. Place 1 tablespoon of butter on each squash half, place in pressure cooker.
2. Sprinkle salt and pepper over squash.
3. Pour the water into pressure cooker; secure lid.
4. Turn pressure cooker on and set timer to 30 minutes.
5. When cook time is complete, and pressure is fully vented, open lid.
6. Serve immediately.

NUTRITION FACTS

Serving Size:
1/4 of a recipe.

Amount Per Serving	% Daily Value
Calories: 177	9%
Calories from Fat: 50	8%
Total Fat: 7g	11%
Saturated Fat: 0g	0%
Cholesterol: 15mg	5%
Sodium: 270mg	11%
Total Carbohydrates: 28g	9%
Fiber: 6g	24%
Sugars: 0g	
Protein: 3g	5%
Vitamin A:	4%
Vitamin C:	0%
Calcium:	0%
Iron:	0%

Spicy Bulgur Pilaf

Servings: 6

INGREDIENTS

1 medium onion, chopped

1 garlic clove, sliced

1 cup bulgur

½ teaspoon turmeric powder

½ teaspoon cumin seeds

1 ½ cups chicken stock

1 tablespoon lemon zest

½ cup black olives

¼ cup lemon juice

1 tablespoon fresh cilantro leaves, chopped

DIRECTIONS

1. Place all ingredients, except cilantro, into the pressure cooker; secure lid.
2. Press vegetable function, add 1 minute; press start.
3. When cook time is complete, and pressure is fully vented, open lid.
4. Fluff using a fork and top with cilantro and serve.

TIP

Bulgur is a healthy and delicious substitute for rice.

NUTRITION FACTS

Serving Size:
1/6 of a recipe.

Amount Per Serving	% Daily Value
Calories: 35	2%
Calories from Fat: 3	0%
Total Fat: 2g	3%
Saturated Fat: 0g	0%
Cholesterol: 0mg	0%
Sodium: 300mg	13%
Total Carbohydrates: 2g	1%
Fiber: 0g	0%
Sugars: 0g	
Protein: 1g	2%
Vitamin A:	0%
Vitamin C:	3%
Calcium:	0%
Iron:	0%

Stuffed Onions

Servings: 4

INGREDIENTS

4 large purple onions

1 tablespoon extra-virgin olive oil

½ pound ground turkey

½ teaspoon salt

½ teaspoon tarragon leaves

2 tablespoons wheat berries

5 apricots, chopped

½ cup white wine

1 cup chicken stock, divided

1 teaspoon white balsamic vinegar

DIRECTIONS

1. Cut the tops and bottoms off the onions then peel off the outer 2 layers.
2. Scoop out the center of each onion until 1-inch is left in the bottom.
3. Press brown/sauté function, add oil and preheat.
4. Add turkey to the pressure cooker and brown for 4 minutes while breaking it up with a wooden spoon; season with salt and tarragon while browning.
5. Add the wheat berries, apricots, wine and ½ cup chicken stock to the pressure cooker cook for 6 minutes, transfer mixture to a bowl.
6. Stuff each onion with the mixture then place the onions in the pressure cooker.
7. Add remaining stock and vinegar into the pressure cooker; secure lid.
8. Press rice function; press start.
9. When cook time is complete, and pressure is fully vented, open lid.
10. Serve onions topped with some remaining stock.

NUTRITION FACTS

Serving Size:
1/4 of a recipe.

Amount Per Serving	% Daily Value
Calories: 150	8%
Calories from Fat: 33	5%
Total Fat: 4g	6%
Saturated Fat: 1g	5%
Cholesterol: 35mg	12%
Sodium: 701mg	29%
Total Carbohydrates: 8g	3%
Fiber: 2g	8%
Sugars: 0g	
Protein: 10g	18%
Vitamin A:	0%
Vitamin C:	20%
Calcium:	0%
Iron:	0%

Sweet Beets and Carrots

Servings: 4

INGREDIENTS

1 pound beets, golden and/or red, peeled and quartered

1 pound carrots, yellow and/or orange, peeled and sliced

½ cup rich chicken stock (see recipe)

½ teaspoon salt

½ teaspoon freshly ground pepper

1 teaspoon lemon zest

1 sprig fresh thyme

2 tablespoons butter

DIRECTIONS

1. Place all ingredients into the pressure cooker; secure lid.
2. Press rice function, minus 2 minutes; press start.
3. When cook time is complete, and pressure is fully vented, open lid.
4. Remove thyme sprig and serve.

NUTRITION FACTS

Serving Size:
1/4 of a recipe.

Amount Per Serving	% Daily Value
Calories: 303	15%
Calories from Fat: 104	16%
Total Fat: 11g	17%
Saturated Fat: 2g	10%
Cholesterol: 103mg	34%
Sodium: 5279mg	220%
Total Carbohydrates: 17g	6%
Fiber: 4g	16%
Sugars: 7g	
Protein: 30g	55%
Vitamin A:	4%
Vitamin C:	87%
Calcium:	3%
Iron:	14%

Szechuan Veggies

Servings: 6

INGREDIENTS

3 cups broccoli florets

3 cups cauliflower florets

1 cup carrot, peeled and sliced

1 red bell pepper, julienned

1 medium onion, thinly sliced

1 tablespoon sesame oil

1 tablespoon water

3 tablespoons oyster sauce

1 teaspoon soy sauce

1 tablespoon fresh ginger, grated

2 garlic cloves, minced

1 teaspoon crushed red pepper flakes

DIRECTIONS

1. Place all ingredients into the pressure cooker; toss well then secure lid.
2. Press fish function; press start.
3. When cook time is complete, and pressure is fully vented, open lid.
4. Serve immediately.

TIP

This is delicious tossed with rice noodles or pasta.

NUTRITION FACTS

Serving Size:
1/6 of a recipe.

Amount Per Serving	% Daily Value
Calories: 57	3%
Calories from Fat: 20	3%
Total Fat: 2g	3%
Saturated Fat: 0g	0%
Cholesterol: 0mg	0%
Sodium: 93mg	4%
Total Carbohydrates: 4g	1%
Fiber: 4g	16%
Sugars: 0g	
Protein: 4g	7%
Vitamin A:	8%
Vitamin C:	186%
Calcium:	5%
Iron:	3%

Tasty Low-Fat Greens

Servings: 4

INGREDIENTS

3 pounds kale, washed, trimmed, and chopped into 2-inch pieces

½ pound smoked turkey, chopped into ½–inch chunks

1 small sweet onion, chopped

½ cup chicken stock

½ teaspoon salt

½ teaspoon smoked paprika

pinch of sugar

DIRECTIONS

1. Place all ingredients into the pressure cooker; stir then secure lid.

2. Press rice function minus 2 minutes; press start.

3. When cook time is complete, and pressure is fully vented, open lid.

4. Serve immediately.

NUTRITION FACTS

Serving Size:
1/4 of a recipe.

Amount Per Serving	% Daily Value
Calories: 95	5%
Calories from Fat: 51	8%
Total Fat: 5g	8%
Saturated Fat: 2g	10%
Cholesterol: 30mg	10%
Sodium: 1124mg	47%
Total Carbohydrates: 1g	0%
Fiber: 0g	0%
Sugars: 0g	
Protein: 10g	18%
Vitamin A:	5%
Vitamin C:	0%
Calcium:	0%
Iron:	2%

Vegetable Curry

Servings: 4

INGREDIENTS

1 medium onion, sliced

1 large sweet potato, peeled and diced

1 medium russet potato, peeled and diced

½ cup chicken stock

1 cup petite diced tomato

1 teaspoon ground cumin

1 teaspoon chili powder

2 teaspoons ground coriander

1 teaspoon turmeric powder

1 cup cauliflower florets

½ cup carrots, peeled and sliced

DIRECTIONS

1. Place all ingredients, except cauliflower and carrots, into the pressure cooker; secure lid.
2. Press fish function; press start.
3. When cook time is complete, and pressure is fully vented, open lid.
4. Add remaining ingredients to the pressure cooker; secure lid.
5. Press fish function; press start.
6. When cook time is complete, and pressure is fully vented, open lid.
7. Serve immediately.

NUTRITION FACTS

Serving Size:
1/4 of a recipe.

Amount Per Serving	% Daily Value
Calories: 100	5%
Calories from Fat: 1	0%
Total Fat: 0g	0%
Saturated Fat: 0g	0%
Cholesterol: 0mg	0%
Sodium: 151mg	6%
Total Carbohydrates: 23g	8%
Fiber: 3g	12%
Sugars: 3g	
Protein: 3g	5%
Vitamin A:	217%
Vitamin C:	32%
Calcium:	1%
Iron:	3%

Warm Potato Salad

Servings: 4

INGREDIENTS

1 pound fingerling potatoes, washed

1 cup champagne vinegar

3 garlic cloves, sliced

1 ½ teaspoons kosher salt

¼ cup peanut oil

3 sprigs fresh parsley

2 teaspoons salt

½ teaspoon black pepper

1 cup water

1 small sweet onion, cut into ¼-inch chunks

3 tablespoons sugar

1 tablespoon fresh thyme leaves, chopped

DIRECTIONS

1. Place potatoes, garlic, parsley, salt, and water into the pressure cooker; secure lid.
2. Press fish function, add 1 minute; press start.
3. While cooking, combine remaining ingredients in a bowl; stir.
4. When cook time is complete, and pressure is fully vented, open lid.
5. Strain the potatoes and let them cool for 20 minutes.
6. Slice the potatoes into ¼-inch thick slices then toss them in the marinade.
7. Let potatoes rest for an additional 20 minutes before serving.

NUTRITION FACTS

Serving Size:
1/4 of a recipe.

Amount Per Serving	% Daily Value
Calories: 221	11%
Calories from Fat: 120	18%
Total Fat: 14g	22%
Saturated Fat: 3g	15%
Cholesterol: 0mg	0%
Sodium: 2070mg	86%
Total Carbohydrates: 24g	8%
Fiber: 1g	4%
Sugars: 10g	
Protein: 2g	4%
Vitamin A:	0%
Vitamin C:	11%
Calcium:	1%
Iron:	3%

Wheat Berry Salad

Servings: 6

INGREDIENTS

1 cup wheat berries, rinsed

2 cups water

½ teaspoon salt

1 small onion, chopped

1 English, cucumber, seeded and chopped

1 medium tomato, diced

½ teaspoon fresh mint leaves, chopped

1 teaspoon lemon juice

½ teaspoon garlic salt

½ teaspoon freshly ground pepper

2 tablespoons extra-virgin olive oil

DIRECTIONS

1. Place wheat berries, water and salt into the pressure cooker; secure lid.
2. Press soup function, add 10 minutes; press start.
3. When cook time is complete, and pressure is fully vented, open lid.
4. Transfer wheat berries to a large bowl; let cool to room temperature.
5. Add remaining ingredients to the bowl; toss well.
6. Chill down 30 minutes before serving.

TIP

Top with crumbled blue cheese.

NUTRITION FACTS

Serving Size:
1/6 of a recipe.

Amount Per Serving	% Daily Value
Calories: 58	3%
Calories from Fat: 40	6%
Total Fat: 5g	8%
Saturated Fat: 1g	5%
Cholesterol: 0mg	0%
Sodium: 387mg	16%
Total Carbohydrates: 3g	1%
Fiber: 0g	0%
Sugars: 0g	
Protein: 1g	2%
Vitamin A:	5%
Vitamin C:	13%
Calcium:	1%
Iron:	1%

Wild Rice with Dried Cranberry and Pecan Stuffing

Servings: 4

INGREDIENTS

1 pound ground turkey

1 small onion, minced

1 celery stalk, chopped

1 teaspoon salt

½ teaspoon freshly ground pepper

1 teaspoon poultry seasoning

1 cup wild rice, rinsed

3 ½ cups chicken stock

½ cup dried cranberries

½ cup dried cranberries

½ cup pecans, chopped

2 sage leaves, chopped

DIRECTIONS

1. Press brown/sauté function, allow to preheat.
2. Add turkey to the pressure cooker; cook for 3 minutes with the lid off while breaking up the turkey using a wooden spoon.
3. Add onions, celery, salt, and pepper to the pressure cooker; cook for an additional 2 minutes while continuing to break up the turkey.
4. Add remaining ingredients to the pressure cooker; secure the lid.
5. Press soup function; press start.
6. When cook time is complete, and pressure is fully vented, open lid.
7. Stir and serve.

TIP

This is a perfect side dish to compliment roast turkey or chicken.

NUTRITION FACTS

Serving Size:
1/4 of a recipe.

Amount Per Serving	% Daily Value
Calories: 520	26%
Calories from Fat: 98	15%
Total Fat: 11g	17%
Saturated Fat: 2g	10%
Cholesterol: 70mg	23%
Sodium: 1272mg	53%
Total Carbohydrates: 64g	21%
Fiber: 6g	24%
Sugars: 24g	
Protein: 25g	45%
Vitamin A:	1%
Vitamin C:	5%
Calcium:	1%
Iron:	4%

Lemon Dill Green Beans

Servings: 6

INGREDIENTS

2 pounds green beans, stems trimmed

¼ cup chicken stock

¼ cup lemon juice

1 teaspoon lemon zest

2 garlic cloves, minced

½ teaspoon salt

½ teaspoon freshly ground pepper

1 tablespoon extra-virgin olive oil

1 teaspoon fresh dill, chopped

DIRECTIONS

1. Place all ingredients into the pressure cooker; secure lid.
2. Press fish function; press start.
3. When cook time is complete, and pressure is fully vented, open lid.
4. Serve immediately.

NUTRITION FACTS

Serving Size:
1/6 of a recipe.

Amount Per Serving	% Daily Value
Calories: 47	2%
Calories from Fat: 20	3%
Total Fat: 2g	3%
Saturated Fat: 0g	0%
Cholesterol: 0mg	0%
Sodium: 690mg	29%
Total Carbohydrates: 5g	2%
Fiber: 3g	12%
Sugars: 3g	
Protein: 1g	2%
Vitamin A:	8%
Vitamin C:	5%
Calcium:	3%
Iron:	5%

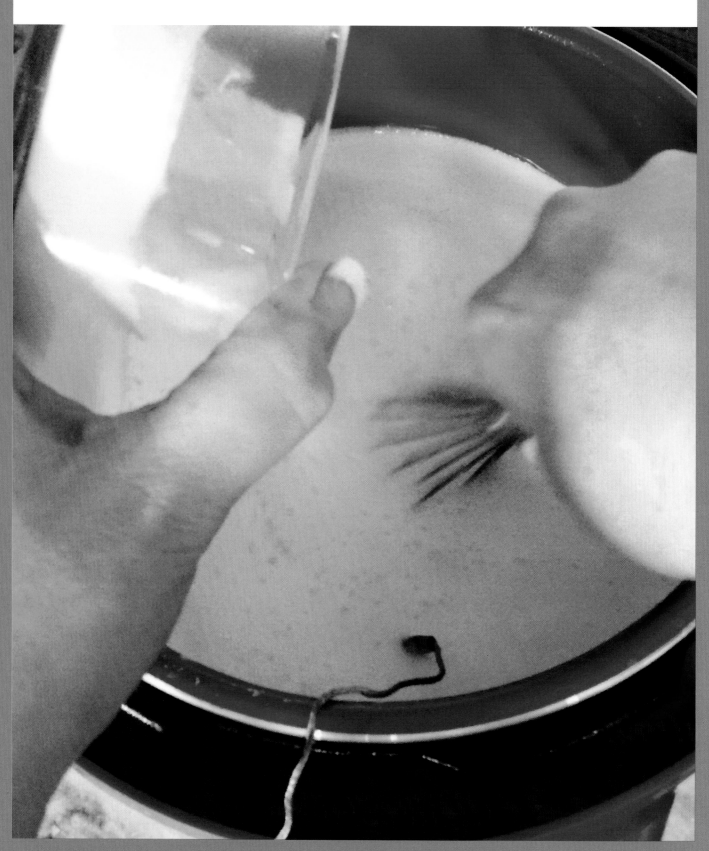

Almond Milk Yogurt
with Chia Seeds

Servings: 4

INGREDIENTS

3 teaspoons chia seeds

culture starter

1 cup whole almonds

2-½ cups purified water

DIRECTIONS

1. Cover almonds with water and soak for 6-8 hours.
2. Strain almonds and place into food processor with the purified water.
3. Strain almond mixture using cheese cloth.
4. Add almond milk to the pressure cooker; secure lid.
5. Press yogurt function; press start.
6. When cook time is complete, about 8 hours, open lid.
7. Store in air-tight containers.

Homemade Yogurt

Yield: 3 quarts

INGREDIENTS

3 quarts whole milk

½ Cup plain yogurt

DIRECTIONS

1. Pour milk into pressure cooker, press brown/sauté function, with lid off bring to a boil, stirring occasionally.

2. Once the milk has come to a boil, turn off heat and let cool to 100-110 degrees, approximately 20 minutes. Make sure milk is cooled, or the heat will kill the bacteria.

3. When milk is cooled to perfect temperature, whisk in yogurt; secure lid

4. Press yogurt function; press start.

5. When cook time is complete, about 8 hours, open lid.

6. Store in air-tight containers.

INDEX

NOTES

NOTES

NOTES